# Up the Main

## Coastal British Columbia Stories

*Wayne J. Lutz*

*Powell River Books*

Note for Librarians: A cataloguing record for this book is available from Library and Archives Canada at www.collectionscanada.ca/amicus/index-e.html
ISBN 1-4120-7218-2

PUBLISHING™

*Offices in Canada, USA, Ireland and UK*

This book was published *on-demand* in cooperation with Trafford Publishing. On-demand publishing is a unique process and service of making a book available for retail sale to the public taking advantage of on-demand manufacturing and Internet marketing. On-demand publishing includes promotions, retail sales, manufacturing, order fulfilment, accounting and collecting royalties on behalf of the author.

**Book sales for North America and international:**
Trafford Publishing, 6E–2333 Government St.,
Victoria, BC v8t 4p4 CANADA
phone 250 383 6864 (toll-free 1 888 232 4444)
fax 250 383 6804; email to orders@trafford.com
**Book sales in Europe:**
Trafford Publishing (uk) Limited, 9 Park End Street, 2nd Floor
Oxford, UK ox1 1hh UNITED KINGDOM
phone 44 (0)1865 722 113 (local rate 0845 230 9601)
facsimile 44 (0)1865 722 868; info.uk@trafford.com
**Order online at:**
trafford.com/05-2113

10 9 8 7 6 5 4 3 2 1

*To Helen, Ed, and their sons...*

*who taught me about Powell River.*
*They represent the many fine families*
*of a community nestled in paradise.*

---

*The stories are true, and the characters are real.*
*Some details are adjusted to protect the guilty.*
*All of the mistakes rest solidly with the author.*

# Acknowledgements

My sincere thanks to the Powell River ATV Club, an organization of varied characters that tolerated me during research for this book. Their attitude ranged from "Oh, here comes the American author," to "Oh, oh, here comes the American author." Much of what the Powell River ATV Club accomplishes includes a generous contribution of new and improved trails for those who bike and hike this beautiful region. They always leave the places they visit better than they find them. But try explaining that to the government authorities. Thus, the names have been (mostly) omitted to protect the innocent.

A quartet of fine women supported me in this project, as they did in my first book. Margy Lutz edited the draft chapters and managed to clean them up before anyone saw how loosely I write. Ellen Straw of Mount San Antonio College's English Department and Irene Miller of Southern Illinois University picked away at the details as my sentence gurus. Quantity has never been my problem in writing. It's the quality thing that gets me. Jeanne Scott of Southern Illinois University continually served as a sounding board for my writing and publishing goals, support that has been both steadfast and essential.

Ed Maithus assisted with the book's artwork, providing cartoons that were far different (and better) than I requested. And, as always, John Maithus led me unceasingly onward to new adventures that carried story after story forward. Without him and his wonderful family (Bro too!), this book would not exist. To the Maithi, I am forever indebted.

*Wayne J. Lutz*
Powell River BC
October 15, 2005

# Contents

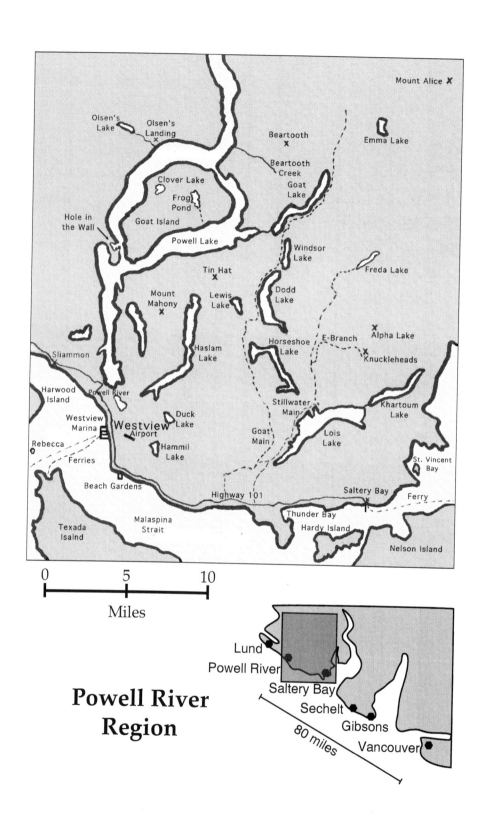

Mount Alice **✗**

Olsen's
Lake
Olsen's
Landing
**✗**

Beartooth
**✗**

Emma Lake

Beartooth
Creek

Clover Lake

Goat
Lake

Frog
Pond

Hole in
the Wall

Goat Island

Powell Lake

Windsor
Lake

Freda Lake

Tin Hat
**✗**

Dodd
Lake

Mount
Mahony
**✗**

Lewis
Lake

Alpha Lake
**✗**

Horseshoe
Lake

E-Branch

Haslam
Lake

Knuckleheads
**✗**

Sliammon

Harwood
Island

Powell River

Stillwater
Main

Khartoum
Lake

Westview
Marina

Westview
Airport

Duck
Lake

Goat
Main

Lois
Lake

Rebecca

Hammil
Lake

St. Vincent
Bay

Ferries

Beach Gardens

Highway 101

Saltery Bay
**✗**

Ferry

Thunder Bay

Texada
Isalnd

Malaspina
Strait

Hardy Island

Nelson Island

0        5        10

Miles

**Powell River
Region**

Lund
Powell River

Saltery Bay

Sechelt

Gibsons

Vancouver

80 miles

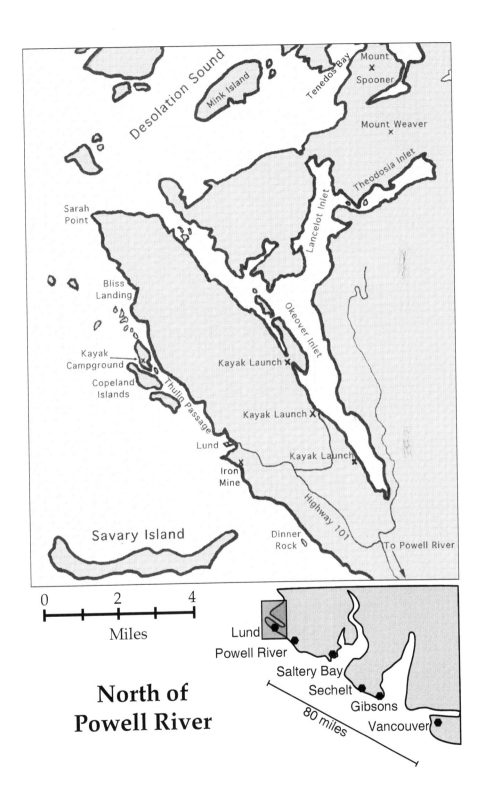

Desolation Sound

Mink Island

Tenedos Bay

Mount Spooner ×

Mount Weaver ×

Lancelot Inlet

Theodosia Inlet

Sarah Point

Bliss Landing

Okeover Inlet

Kayak Campground ×

Kayak Launch ×

Copeland Islands

Thulin Passage

Kayak Launch ×

Lund

Kayak Launch ×

Iron Mine ×

Highway 101

Savary Island

Dinner Rock

To Powell River

0          2          4

Miles

# North of
# Powell River

Lund

Powell River

Saltery Bay

Sechelt

Gibsons

Vancouver

80 miles

## Preface

## After *Up the Lake*

*Up the Main* is a companion volume to *Up the Lake*, focusing on stories of ATV exploration in the Powell River area of British Columbia. It also includes two of my favorite topics, life on Powell Lake and boating in the Strait of Georgia.

A dilemma from *Up the Lake* involved the need to cut some of my favorite chapters to allow the original volume to be offered at an acceptable price. Thus, some chapters in *Up the Main* may be recognized as a continuation of *Up the Lake* themes. Ideally, the reader will pursue these two volumes in order. But, in reality, the books (and even the chapters) can be read in any order.

*Up the Lake* ended with a telephone conversation with John regarding the new firewood float. I wasn't sure what to expect when I arrived at my float cabin on the next visit. Not surprisingly, John didn't let me down.

\* \* \* \* \*

In late November, I angle my way into the Hole in the Wall, the Campion at near-idle. I try to absorb the ever-supernatural scenery. It is late evening, and the shadows have drawn themselves over the Hole in the Wall.

The changes are the first things to grasp my attention. The firewood float appears off the bow, as anticipated, moored to the inside of the breakwater. The silver metal roof of the open-air floating shed has a slight slope, a John-design to handle the snow (but not tonight). Large hand-painted lettering, illegible from this distance, dominates the lower plywood walls. A remnant of John's construction? Graffiti in remote tranquility?

As I pass abeam the cabin, the Bayliner comes into view, riding smartly in the water behind Cabin Number 3. Both VHF antennas have been lowered nearly horizontal, making the boat look wounded. John has a reason, I'm sure.

I swing around the breakwater logs and enter my arbitrary floating property line. The Hole has sucked the remaining daylight from the air, as my halogen docking lights flash against the firewood float. On this side, the lower plywood wall of the shed sports a combination of large red and green hand-painted letters, now readable, although upside-down:

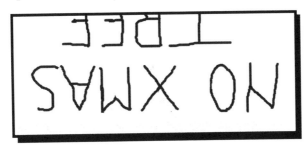

It's a classic firewood float, with John's construction character included. As I swing past the new float, I need to concentrate on docking in the darkness, but I can't resist stealing a glance over my shoulder to inspect the lettering on the other side. In the fading light, I can barely read the letters on the split plywood sign. This section is right-side-up:

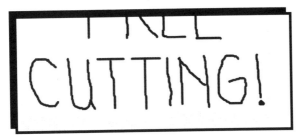

Nothing is wasted. That's the First-Rule-of-John. The plywood markings fit naturally into the character of Cabin Number 3. I am home.

# Chapter 1

## Mud and Guts

"There's a deer in the parking lot," I state to the clerk with a sense of accusation, almost hostility.

A deer in a parking lot is not particularly noteworthy in Powell River, but this deer is made out of plastic, about four-feet high.

I hit the brakes as I approached the store, just in time to make the turn into the parking lot. I knew that something was wrong, and I needed an answer. The molded black bear is gone, and there could be no good news in this regard. I'm sorry, but a foo-foo deer just isn't an adequate replacement for the black bear that has watched over this parking lot for years.

The teenage clerk refuses to look me in the eye. She probably has faced this situation many times already today. I can't tell whether her sad face and near-tears are real.

"It was a hit-and-run," says the girl. "Bruno is in three pieces in the back room."

"A hit-'n-run?!" The clerk probably wonders whether I'm really upset. I can put on a pretty good act, but this time it's real.

"Poor Bruno," I relent. "Is he really dead, or can Sam put him back together?" It's probably a common question.

"We're not sure yet. But it's pretty bad."

I'm tempted to ask if I can see the damage, but it wouldn't be pleasant to see Bruno in pieces. I thank the clerk (sincerely) for the report. It's probably not fair to complain about the deer. But a deer could never replace a bear. When we're quadding, we'll stop and watch deer. They're a calming sight, and I always manage a smile when I see them. But a bear – now there's an animal to watch. All quads grind to a halt, and we intently follow the bear until it is completely out of sight. We might crank up and leave while a deer is still lingering in the field.

I've only been in town for three days. I've passed this parking lot several times already, and I've observed Bruno chained to his spot. (The chain I accept – I can see why a lot of pranksters would want this bear.) He stands (used to stand) right next to the Fish-O-Meter, indicating the status of the local salmon catch. Of course, I've never noticed the Fish-O-Meter's needle in the "Low" range. It's always at least in the bottom of the "Moderate" zone, although there have been some pretty bad salmon dry spells in the area. A low fishing meter doesn't sell anything, so that little white lie is acceptable. But a hit-and-run – it makes you think twice about this town.

\* \* \* \* \*

John has already heard about Bruno. He doesn't miss a thing.

Right now, I am trying to act enthused about his new purchase. I knew it was coming, because he has been talking about it for over a year. He has craved a camcorder, and now he has purchased one. I figure it is the end of life, as we know it. Our trips into the forests are unspoiled. What can a camcorder do to improve things? It'll all go downhill from here. Already I am dreading this weekend's trip into Theodosia.

I've watched friends adopt camcorders, and their lives change. They get carried away with filming and lose sight of the event. It changes things. What's wrong with keeping vivid memories in your mind? John is a perfectionist, and a camcorder in the hands of a perfectionist is even worse. It will be endless editing and reediting. He'll have us stop as we prepare to climb up a trail with our quads. John will need to position himself in the perfect spot, and then we'll climb the trail as if no one is filming. Sure.

I saw it coming, and I tried to stop it. But when John makes up his mind about something, it's gonna happen. I remember the day in Dan's shop before John bought his quad. He showed me a framed photo mounted on the wall. The Powell River ATV Club posed for a picture overlooking a deep valley. It could have been an advertisement for Yamaha, with all the quads lined up. The photo was so clear that you could read the bear model names on the bikes: Grizzly, Kodiak, Bruin.

"Look at those guys," says John. "Ain't that some photo?"

"Yes, it is," I reply, trying to act interested in a recreational activity that doesn't tweak my interest in the least.

"Now look close at that photo," says John. "Do you notice one little detail that's missing?"

I scan the photo carefully. John is big on details, and I am trying to see what is missing.

"No, I don't see it," I admit.

"Me. That's what's missing – me,"

John is right. He isn't in that photo. But there is no stopping him. He has to have a quad. But not me – that's something I'm sure I will never want.

* * * * *

**I** meet John to load the quads on Saturday morning. His brothers will converge on Theodosia from several different locations. Rick is coming off a night shift in the taxicab, but that doesn't bother him. He drives almost on autopilot and is one of the best riders in coastal BC. Dave is doubling on his quad with his wife, Jayne, and quads are new to him. Doubling is not easy in tough terrain, so I'm expecting that I won't be the laggard today. I've been into Theodosia three times previously, and I've already challenged my riding skills on today's route on a smaller quad without four-wheel drive (*Up the Lake*, Chapter 12). Today's ride on an almost-new Kodiak 450 should be child's play by comparison. I've come a long way in a year.

It would be wonderful if we could get John's third bother to join us today. All four brothers have never ridden simultaneously, so maybe the camcorder actually would have a purpose. I would like to help film that event. I suggest to John that we invite Rob to join us, but John's phone calls to Rob go unanswered. He's probably working his taxicab today.

Jimmy will be joining us too. He's a quad rider who proves that you never age if you just keep riding. We'll all converge on Theodosia via the same road, but we all have separate preferences regarding our off-load locations.

My quad is stored at Rob's house (gotta get a garage soon). When we arrive, Rob is dangling out of the kitchen window, waving to us with his portable taxi dispatch radio. I have a present for him (a T-shirt from the States), so I hand it up to him through the open window.

"Come riding with us," I order. "They'll think your radio has gone dead and not even miss you."

Rob laughs, seems to consider it for a moment, and then says: "Maybe not today."

"Thanks for taking care of my stuff," I say. Rob's garage has become a storage area for way-too-many things, but he never seems to mind.

"No worries," he retorts.

John opens the garage door, and we attempt to extract my quad, wedged between a wheelbarrow, Rob's trailered boat, and another quad that belongs to my wife. I ask John to make the first start of the season for my quad and drive it up onto the homemade utility trailer (deftly crafted by John from a trailer that came with my tin boat). I'm not sure I remember where the starter button is located.

✱ ✱ ✱ ✱ ✱

**D**ave is already off-loaded when we pull up behind his pickup truck just off Highway 101. Jayne is testing out a bandana – it's still early June, but the road dust will already be a problem, even with the recent rains. John waits for me to start my quad and drive it off the trailer, but I defer to him to off-load my bike – I don't want to embarrass myself in front of Dave and Jayne. As I remind Dave, there was a recent incident (he heard about it, of course) where I rammed John's tailgate during my attempt to drive my quad onto the trailer. If you saw John's truck, you'd wonder why there was so much chagrin over such an incident. But John insisted on having a body shop restore the tailgate of his rusting truck to its like-old condition.

When it is finally time to get riding, John is away in a flash. I'm still fumbling with the starter switch, and nothing is happening. Not only is nothing happening, but absolutely nothing is working properly. I can't find neutral, I've lost a glove, and the zipper on my jacket is jammed. Dave is patiently waiting for me, knowing that I am, from his standpoint, the weak link today.

"It's dead, Dave," I announce, after making sure I've tried everything.

"Here, move that red electrical cutoff switch to "On," he says.

"Oh." Vroom, vroom – she starts smartly on the first crank. I can't wait for the camcorder action.

The dust-length is about a quarter-mile today, and I am between John and Dave. But it will take awhile to catch up with John (and Bro in his aft-mounted dog throne), so I have an excuse to cruise at 50 klicks on the dirt road. Potholes are difficult to see in advance in the mix of sun and trees, so I take them with a solid thump before I am able to slow or maneuver around them.

I catch up with John, parked and waiting at the widened dirt area near the bridge. This bridge has been closed for nearly a year, with the few residents on the other side getting plenty grumpy. They have to park their vehicles on their side of the bridge, walk across the condemned structure, usually carrying a heavy load, and drive to town in a vehicle stored on the other side. It's a slow and demanding portage of about 200 feet, including the barricaded approaches to the bridge on each side. Quads and motorcylcles – we refer to both as "bikes" – can make it across, between the huge cement blocks, but you can see paint on the cement where they have cut it a little close. (One month later, a new bridge is built here, and it is completed in less than three weeks, an amazingly short period of time, considering the challenge of the terrain.)

At the bridge, Jimmy is off-loading his quad and trying to strap sheets of plywood and a small outboard motor to his bike. The plywood is for the raft awaiting us at the lake – the floorboards need refurbishment. None of us are pleased with Jimmy's load, since it seems obvious it will hang up on tight trail corners and slow us down. John helps Jimmy load the plywood and strap it onto the rear rack. None of us complain about the 2.5 horse outboard motor that is strapped to the front.

Rick joins us at the bridge, while John and Jimmy wrestle with the plywood, and now Jayne (with Dave riding double behind her) arrives on the Kodiak. John wants this to be the first footage with his camcorder, but he isn't ready for their arrival, so he asks Jayne and Dave to go back and return for some action shots. Oh, great – this will be interesting – two people arriving at a bridge parking area on a quad (staged shots, no less). I'm convinced the camcorder is the end of our carefree wilderness life.

We're ready to go now, maneuvering our quads across the condemned bridge in sequence. It's the order we will ride most of the day. John leads, followed by Jimmy, then Rick, then me, and finally Dave with Jayne doubling on the back. Grizz, Grizz, Kodiak, Kodiak.

We approach the stop sign at a remote dirt road intersection. Did someone put that sign here for special effect? We roar through the intersection after slowing a bit, with a quick look both ways. The road turns into a trail, and the trail becomes a wide wet path. It is a mix of rocks and mud but only a moderate challenge that hardly slows us down. And the dust is gone.

Our climb into Theodosia is just as scenic as I always remember it, but it is much less challenging than that first time. In fact, it is a breeze, and I realize I have come a long way with my riding skills – once I figure out how to get 'er started. But John has stopped to get some shots of us climbing the hill, and it's all messed up. None of us know that John is preparing to film the climb, so we just blast through while he is getting the camera out of his quad box.

Now we are on top of the ridge on the wide logging road that leads into Theodosia. Everything has changed.

You'd think that trails would change little in an area like this, but logging is an ever-changing operation, with new areas being cut every day. We reach the previously blocked entrance to the descent into Theodosia, and there is a gap in the boulder pile wide enough for a quad. John and his friends decided to unpile the boulders one more time to see if the loggers would retaliate. They didn't.

We descend on the rugged trail into the valley, roll out onto the wide logging road, and are cruising smoothly towards our destination – a raft and a June day that should be full of trout. There is one brief stop as we encounter a logging crew removing what remains of a large logging truck from the ditch beside the road. The truck has completely overturned. A giant logging crane makes quick work of the cleanup, the road is clear, and we're on our way again.

The approach to the trail to the lake is completely different than I remember from my previous trip. A giant logging slash is our point of entry, finally joining with the previous year's narrow trail. I'm pleased that we don't have to traverse the difficult path across the inlet that harbors tightly-crowded alders constantly overgrowing the trail. Soon we are through the scenic part and into the mud.

Although my first trip to this lake was difficult on the smaller two-wheel-drive quad, this trip is even more challenging on the mightier Kodiak. The mud and ruts make the difference. The lower reaches of the trail are flooded, and the ruts are deep. Everyone gets stuck, even John. I've never seen John have to back up at an obstacle, but he does it twice today. We all wallow in the mud, get stranded on rocks and logs, and bottom-out at various spots on the route. All of us, that is, except Rick. His expertise at traversing the most difficult of terrain is legendary. He flies over the obstacles rather than drives over them.

I am amazed at how well Dave makes it through. He has less quad-hours than me, but his background in off-road motorcycles shows that ATV skills are universal, no matter how you cut it. With Jayne on the back, it is even more challenging, but Dave makes it through tough spots in fine shape, with one major bout in a severe rut that takes him four reverse-then-forward tries to extract his quad.

As for me, I do pretty well. One corner finds me stranded on top of a log, my bulletproof oil pan lodged firmly on the crest of the obstacle. Everyone is yelling instructions at me, and I treat the onlookers to a terrible grinding noise as I pop out of low gear while trying to abide by John's orders to "Give 'er shit!" It is all captured by John's videocam, of course.

One benefit of the video recording is the need for John to occasionally stop to get set up for the rest of us to come through the trail. John doesn't normally like to stop on the trail, and I'm never displeased to have a break from riding. So there are some advantages today. Every instance of particularly severe trail conditions is met with an order from John to "Wait up," while he gets in position for movie action. I take advantage of these Hollywood moments to catch my breath.

Jimmy encounters a lot of frustration with his plywood cargo on the narrow trail. The sheets of plywood catch on trees during corners, ripping the bungee cords from his rear rack. That requires repeated stops to secure his load. We begin the trek with all but Jimmy annoyed about the plywood. Now he too is swearing at it.

The final descent into the small lake valley is easy in comparison to the muddy ruts. Pulling into the lake turnaround area, I am exhausted. It goes immediately to my stomach, and I gulp down a roast beef sandwich and a half tub of supermarket potato salad.

Jayne starts a fire, and Dave roasts hotdogs. John is videotaping the non-action in the camping area. This is a campsite that John and his friends have personally constructed. The nearby raft has been built from scratch and is stored, tied to a log, a few hundred feet from the campground.

John and I (Bro included, of course) head for the raft, install the outboard motor on the transom, and relocate this fine vessel to the campsite. Jimmy and John go to work right away refurbishing the raft's logs with the plywood. Without this renovation, the raft would not be able to hold today's group. In fact, launch of the raft should not have been attempted with today's heavy load, even with the overhauled floor.

Five of us (six, including Bro) motor and pole our way around the lake for several hours. Rick volunteers to stay ashore, minding the campfire and blazing his typical trail improvements near the campsite. The raft probably could not have held another body anyway. We are barely above the waterline, and sometimes below it. Bro moves around unexpectedly, requiring us to immediately redistribute our weight to prevent sinking. We are usually standing, sometimes sharing the two stump seats.

The fishing is great. Jayne catches the first trout, and we use it as bait to attract more fish. Everybody catches at least one trout, and several fish are well over a pound. We also catch a lot of underwater logs. Captain John maneuvers the outboard motor (which barely pushes the overloaded vessel) every-which-way to retrieve our lures. At one location in the shallow water, three of us are simultaneously hung up on different obstacles. We don't lose a single lure.

As we return to the campsite, we begin laughing about how this would look from shore (if there were people to observe). Five people and a dog are crowded onto this small raft, and we are riding so low that we must look like we are standing on the water.

Rick uses the videocam to capture our return to the campsite. We regroup to gather our gear and begin the slow journey back to civilization. All goes fairly well, punctuated by numerous hang-ups in the mud and ruts. I am in low gear and four-wheel drive constantly.

At one of our brief stops, I hear John announce that we'll make one more stop at the point near the logging camp. I'm not sure where the point is, but everyone nods. The logging camp is not a big place, so I simply put my helmet back on and begin the final leg.

After we return to the main logging road, I linger about a half-mile behind Rick to keep out of his dust. I know Dave is behind me, so there is no need to worry about getting lost. I blast into the logging camp at about 50 klicks and continue to the end of the road, where the climb out of the valley begins. No one is there.

Could they have started out of the valley without me? The route is so clear at this point that John might have decided to simply press on. But I should wait for Dave to be sure all is okay with him. And so I wait. And wait.

I turn my engine off to conserve fuel and enjoy the quiet. I prop my feet up on the front fenders, and immediately I hear the blast of John's horn. He must have been listening to my engine, waiting for it to quit so that I would hear his horn.

It doesn't sound like he is very far away, but he is definitely back along the way I have come. I hit the starter, shift into gear, and off I go on the logging road. I'm trying to watch the road for ruts and rocks, but I'm also glancing left and right to find John's location. I've traveled about a mile now, and that seems further than the horn's location. Suddenly, there is a roar, as Dave passes me, motioning without gentleness that I should turn around and follow him. I feel like a guilty driver being stopped by a cop.

As I turn onto the road to the point, I follow Dave along the short trail that leads to the rest of our group. They are laughing and pointing at me. I immediately turn off my engine.

"Hey, you guys," I yell matter-of-factly. "You were all really lost. You're just lucky I was able to find you."

There are some derogatory comments about Americans, but all is well again.

During the climb out of Theodosia, we encounter a large bear, foraging solo near the road in the logging slash. We stop and watch until the bear exits into the forest above the slash. Bro is howling at the top of his lungs the whole time, and it is a good thing he is too rotund to jump out of his quad box and chase the bear. This is the second bear we have spotted today. (Dave and Jayne saw a third).

As soon as we get started again, we see three more bears crowded around a tree, seemingly trying to escape our inspection. The mother and her two tiny cubs (the smallest I have ever seen) finally dart upward out of the slash into the protection of the forest. Bro is howling, and John's camcorder is rolling.

By sunset, we are home.

* * * * *

John and I off-load my quad at Rob's house and haul the empty trailer through the take-out entrance at A & W. I'm not sure John will be able to make the tight corner at the end of the "Dub" drive-through, but he negotiates the curve successfully. We get our chicken, fries, and root beer, and cruise on back to John's house. I am totally exhausted, and my fatigue is just starting to sink in.

"Don't forget the video," says John.

I'd like to.

"I shot 52 minutes," he says. That's fifty-two minutes of agony, so we might as well get it over with.

We prop ourselves up in front of the television, with John's parents and Rick filling the remaining seats. John's dad, Ed, is at least as negative about this as I am. He asks whether we really need to interrupt a good movie on Canadian TV for this silliness. Rick sits without comment, going smoothly with the flow, as always. I'm glad I have my chicken from the "Dub" to distract me.

The first minute of video is Dave and Jayne arriving at the entrance to the old bridge. Ed comments sarcastically: "That's pretty exciting." There's only 51 minutes left.

The next 10 minutes involve John trying to hold the camera steady while he navigates down the trail into Theodosia. There is only the ground immediately in front of the quad in the frame, and it bounces around a lot. You can barely hear John's voice describing the route over the roar of the engine.

"What are you saying?" asks Ed. John doesn't answer and refuses to fast-forward through the 10 minutes of bouncing ground. No one is impressed, except John.

Now we are in the mud and ruts, and more mud, and stuck quads, and gunning engines, and horrible crunching noises. And suddenly, I start to get interested. We were there? It looks even tougher on the videotape than in person. Wheels are spinning and mud is flying. I'm stuck on top of a log, and then there's the loud scream of my slipped gearshift. Everybody laughs. John's dad says: "Wow!" And he means it.

John's mother, Helen, comments: "I never realized this is the kind of trails you ride on?" She looks more than a little shocked.

"You're crazy," says Ed. "Look at these people. Why in hell would they put so much effort into trying to get to a little lake?" He loves it now. So do I.

Engines are roaring and everybody is stuck. We're blasting through mud. Our quads are bouncing every-which-way. In one scene, John has handed the camera to Rick, and now we watch John and Bro thrashing through the obstacle course. Bro is shifting his weight from side to side, holding on for dear life. We ride behind John and see this all the time. John has never seen Bro riding in his quad box. John loves it.

In another scene, we are all stopped, engines off. A tree has fallen across the trail, and Rick is tearing through the log with his chainsaw. Sawdust is flying, and the saw screams.

We're all laughing now. This is a totally agonizing journey that even we, as riders, didn't realize was quite this demanding.

Now the engine noise is gone, and we are standing around the campfire at the lake. Rick is kicked back on the side of the hill, looking totally bored but content. There's the raft, ready to go. But the next frame is a time leap, as Rick picks up the camera when we are returning from our fishing trip. The raft is in the distance but slowly growing in size. And on it are five people and a dog, mostly standing, huddled together and shifting their weight. You can barely see the raft. It looks like these five idiots (exclude the dog) are standing on the water with sticks in their hands. John's mother starts laughing, and she can't stop. I am gasping for air, and Ed is roaring too.

Now there's more mud and roaring engines and quads stuck in the ruts.

"Look at those idiots!" laughs Ed. "It looks like a war zone. Mud and guts." He's right – it is a bit like a muddy war.

As we leave Theodosia, there are tiny bear cubs, scampering with their mother to safety. In the background is Bro's ugly, persistent howling, like a fire truck's siren in the forest.

And then there's one final set of frames as my quad goes ripping through the logging camp in a roar of dust (50 klicks worth). The distant engine slows to idle and runs for a few more minutes, as voices in the background say interesting things about Americans. The quad motor silences, and you can hear John's loud horn only a few feet from the camera. The distant motor starts up again. Another cloud of dust in the opposite direction, right past the logging point again. There goes Dave, roaring after the cloud of dust.

Ed is howling, Helen is howling, I'm gagging and laughing, John is beaming from ear to ear, and Rick is smiling.

I guess John's camcorder won't put an end to our wilderness adventures, after all.

# Chapter 2

# Winding Down (and Up)

When I land at Powell River Airport, via Pacific Coastal or my Piper Arrow, my mental adjustment is major but almost immediate. The change of pace from Los Angeles is extreme, but the adjustment is soothing. As I drive down the hill from the airport, the modification of my attitude is complete the moment I sight the chuck.

In the other direction, arriving in Los Angeles, the adjustment is completely different. Winding down is quick and simple. Winding up is a major battle.

Recognizing that Los Angeles International Airport is one of the busiest transportation facilities in the world and that I often arrive on a Sunday evening or at the end of a school recess (busy travel periods), there should be no surprise. The pace is frantic.

I step off the curb and a horn honks. I finally make it to my car, and I enter traffic that I have not seen for weeks or months. Everyone battles the traffic, but I battle the change – winding up. Usually I wind up too fast. By the first freeway interchange, I am swearing at the other drivers as they speed past, weaving in and out. Undoubtedly, these same drivers are swearing at me – slow poke.

Upon returning to Los Angeles, I avoid people and technology as much as possible for the first 24 hours. Usually by the end of that period I am sadly in the groove of the city. I bustle around the streets doing mundane errands and fitting in quite well, as observed from the outside. Inside, I long to be in Powell River.

The telephone and my pile of awaiting mail are often the biggest problems when it comes time to wind up. Satellite phone technology allows me to make essential calls from my float cabin, with no capability of receiving incoming calls. (That's what I tell others – it isn't true, but my satellite phone remains off except when I elect to make a call, supposedly to conserve battery power.)

The lack of incoming calls on the float is vastly different from a ringing telephone in Los Angeles. I don't have to answer the phone in California and seldom do, but its ring is an interruption to my privacy that is not sacrificed in the least on my float.

The amount of junk mail that accumulates in my absence is amazing. I don't think we recognize how much of this stuff we receive daily until we let it build up for a month. Filtering it from the important mail (bills that are approaching overdue) is a chore. I try to leave the mail alone for at least 24 hours too.

Gradually, over a few days, I fully acclimate to the city. I refuse to forget what I have left behind in Canada, but the city absorbs me. Within a week, it seems that coastal BC is only alive in my imagination. On U.S. television, the Weather Channel logo blocks out the Sunshine Coast completely.

*  *  *  *  *

**W**inding down upon arrival in Powell River is aided by a preliminary stop elsewhere in Canada. Flying on airlines, that stop is Vancouver. Via Piper Arrow, the stop is typically Boundary Bay or Nanaimo to clear customs. These stops have enough of the Canadian flavor to initiate the winding down process.

Of course, Vancouver International is no Powell River, but it is a reminder that I am almost there. The Pacific Coastal bus ride to the slower-paced South Terminal is a step in the right direction, and then the Sunshine Coast is below me as I fly the last leg of the journey. The familiarity of the nooks and crannies of the coastline is a great transition to the final winding down process.

*  *  *  *  *

**P**owell River attitudes that are dramatically distinct from Los Angeles mind-sets include the overall pace of life and a different sense of priorities. Local concerns regarding subsistence needs are high, but it is also a matter of respect for the basic qualities of life. Take eating, for example.

On an almost-hot summer day I arrive at John's Number 1 cabin to find a crowd of guests. John is always congenial regarding visitors, and his float fills with friends on hot summer weekends. If you are looking for a water wonderland, John is always ready to invite you aboard. The crowds bother me, especially when I am hoping for a discussion with John regarding a new project or an idea I entertain while motoring up the lake or southbound from my cabin.

On this particular day, there are no boat parking spots remaining at Number 1, even though John's cabin has lots of boat docks. So I pull in front of the cabin and toss a rope to John's brother, Rob. A young child with a set of yellow inflated water wings jumps off the deck right next to my still-moving boat. His dad appears around the corner, yelling at the kid to get back aboard the float.

"Just tie me up anywhere," I say. "I'm only going to be a minute."

"Here, that will do for now," says Rob, tying my line to a float beam.

"Could you do me a favor, Rob? Would you ask John to come out here to talk with me for just a minute? I've got something private to discuss, and maybe we can do it in my boat."

"Sure," says Rob, and he walks away to find John.

There is no doubt where John is located. He always sits on the porch in his favorite chair, like a king holding court. His float could be burning down as his crowd of friends frolic on the deck, and he would still sit there calmly issuing firefighting instructions.

Today, as I pulled past the porch, I waved to John as he sat in his expected location, just out of sight from where I am now parked. I know John won't mind coming over to the boat. I really don't want to deal with the other people on the float this day (good people), since what I want to discuss is a bit personal.

Rob returns to my boat: "John says he ain't coming out. He's eatin' dinner."

This I understand, within reason, but I am insistent. I know he is eating in his favorite chair on the other side of the cabin. That's important, but so is this.

"John!" I yelled kiddingly. "Get out here! I've got something I need to discuss."

"I'm busy!" he yells back.

"Johnny!" I yell. Then I turn to Rob and ask him if anyone ever calls John by the name Johnny.

"Not if you have any sense," says Rob.

"Johnny! Hey, Johnny!" I yell. No response.

Finally I give in to the situation and hop aboard the float, dodging another young child within a too-large inner tube, leaping off the deck. I walk around the side of the cabin to find John. As expected, he is in his chair on the porch, with several plates of food on a small table in front of him – barbecued chicken, tater tots, and green beans. John smiles at me.

"I'm right in the middle of dinner," he says. "Have some."

I grab a tater tot and dip it in the splattering of ketchup on the edge of the "tots" plate. Bro sits next to John, taking occasional bites of the chicken from the platter. John holds a chicken breast firmly so that the dog can get a piece of it without disappearing with the whole thing.

"Green beans?" I ask in amazement. "That's a vegetable." John doesn't eat vegetables.

"I'm trying to eat healthier," he replies. "Beans aren't so bad, as long as there is water handy to wash them down, like pills."

John places food at a very high priority. Nothing interrupts his meals, and that's the way it should be.

\* \* \* \* \*

This town has its wonders and its standard frustrations. There is actually a rush hour on Joyce Avenue these days. Fortunately, it only lasts a few minutes, unless it's the result of the ferry just arriving or shift change at the paper mill. But with few stoplights, trying to get across Joyce during rush hour can be a frustration.

Life is full of frustrations. But what counts as a frustration in Los Angeles is not what counts in a town like Powell River.

One afternoon, I am motoring down the lake to get to town for some groceries. I need to meet John soon, and I am running late. But approaching Shinglemill, the gas gauge is getting low. It always seems that getting gas is easier when I arrive than when I depart the docks, so now is the time to do it, even though I am running late.

I reduce power to the standard no-wake speed for the Campion (call it low-wake with the dual props), and head for the gas dock. There is usually limited parking space at this dock, with some of the space temporarily taken by boats using the launch ramp. A weekday afternoon like today should cut down on that traffic, so I expect a smooth arrival.

As I round the corner to position myself for the gas dock, "Damn!" I say out loud. There's a floatplane tied to the gas dock, and it's facing in toward the pumps, hogging most of the space. This airplane doesn't take marine fuel, so its pilot is probably just parked so he can go to the pub for lunch. Now I'll have to park at the alternate fuel dock – not a problem really, but a little more effort.

So let's review the problem – a floatplane is parked in front of the pub, tying up part of the gas dock. Now that's a real tension-producer. In Los Angeles, there is cause for road rage on every mile of the freeway every hour of the day. Everything has to be evaluated in perspective. I laugh at myself, consciously relax a bit, and gas up my boat while admiring the Cessna on floats.

\* \* \* \* \*

Jess is one of the characters on the lake. His float is within sight of mine, and Jess lives for his visits to his cabin. He built the cabin from scratch in his back yard. Considering its tiny size, that wasn't a bad idea. As a kid, he told everyone that he wanted to have a float cabin on the lake someday, and he never stopped pursuing his dream. The cabin is so small ("Eight by ten, just like a picture," he proudly says) that he barely has room for a bed and stove inside, but he somehow packs a whole home in 80 square feet.

When Jess finished building his cabin, he hoisted it onto his truck and proceeded to drive it to the dock for towing by boat to the Hole in the Wall. As he left his driveway, a local parade was in progress (in Powell River, beauty queens are the only custom more plentiful than parades), so he wound between the parade vehicles and the marching band, making his way to the dock. He was the hit of the parade.

When Jess is on his float, he is in constant motion. He uses a small fiberglass open boat to bounce around in once he arrives with his primary boat (only slightly larger). He bought his bounce-around boat for only $75, and he has the right to beat it to death.

Jess has been working on his log breakwater lately, pushing and pulling logs around to new positions with this open boat, revving his outboard engine to full-throttle, until it sounds like it is going to hemorrhage. The floating breakwater doesn't seem to change a bit, but he keeps at it all afternoon. Then he hops into his go-home boat and is gone.

*\* \* \* \* \**

**F**lying with John is always a unique experience. Usually it is only a round-trip to Vancouver to drop my wife, Margy, at the airport, but we've done some longer cross-countries too. Not surprisingly, he's interested in airplane technology, but would prefer a floatplane or helicopter over a Piper Arrow. I fly high and city-like, usually on instrument flight rules, and he constantly suggests that I "take 'er down low so we can see something." That's not my style of flying, so often we fly together anticipating different adventures. He enjoys the flying but approaches it with less interest than I would have guessed.

On one visit to Vancouver International Airport to drop Margy for an airline flight home, we receive a ringside seat during refueling.

Wide-body airliners are coming and going at a frantic pace. One of the major runways is closed for construction, thus constricting all takeoffs to a single runway. Margy gives us a surprise present as she departs in her taxi for the international terminal – two huge slices of pizza that she purchased at the local coffee shop. John and I are always ready to eat, so this will be a nice snack for the flight home.

As we depart the parking ramp in the Arrow, the ground control frequency is crowded as everyone heads for the same runway. We complete our pre-takeoff checks and pull up to the runway, number four in line for departure at this intersection. I explain to John that it would be best to cease our private intercom communications until we are safely out of the traffic pattern, since there is a lot going on, and I need to hear our departure sequence and instructions. John fully understands, and the voices through our headsets are now only those of pilots and controllers trying to sort out the mess.

Air traffic control gets us airborne rather quickly, considering the circumstances – sandwiched between a departing Airbus 340 and an arriving Boeing 747, two giant jets. At about 200 feet, I reach over to retract the landing gear. As the gear is coming up, John speaks for the first time since our mutually agreed upon silence.

"Hey, Wayne." John has a way of saying this that tells you he has an important concern.

"Yes, John," I reply, as I busily trim the nose pitch, reduce the manifold pressure, reset the prop RPM, and lean the mixture.

"Do you think it would be okay to eat that pizza now?"

We pull out the pizza slices and munch happily as air traffic control continues to go crazy. We weave our way out of busy Vancouver International, toward the quieter skies of Powell River.

# Chapter 3

## In the Rearview Mirror

I pull into John's driveway and find him bent over the trailer. Better described – he is bent over one of the many trailers in his yard. This particular trailer is a small utility trailer for a single quad, and it has an obvious flat tire. The threads on the wheel bolts are rusted, and John is wrenching on the remains.

"Slow leak around the rim," he says, as he wrestles the first bolt free. "I've got a spare around here somewhere."

I assist him with the heavy hydraulic jack, as he moves it into position. The jack would be able to support a logging truck. After the wheel is removed, I follow John behind the house where three storage sheds are nestled side-by-side. He walks up to an open shed and glances down at a plethora of wheels in a variety of sizes. With as many trailers as reside here, you need a variety of spare wheels.

"There it is." It looks brand new, with the wheel painted white and the tire hard with air. "We'll swap it now, and I'll fix the old one later." You always need a spare.

As I watch him complete the wheel replacement, we discuss the morning's schedule. I am in town briefly for some book business, and John is supposed to join me for the 15-mile ride to the Saltery Bay ferry terminal to post an advertisement on the bulletin board. We also plan to walk the new scenic "tourist" trail at the bay, only because I insist. We'll be back in town in only a few hours, and I'll be headed up the lake by early afternoon.

John lowers the jack and turns to me with that mischievous gleam in his eyes. He wiggles his right thumb in a flexing motion in front of my face, and I give him my squinting "What's this?" look. He flexes his thumb again, waiting for me to catch on.

"Nice day for riding," says John, wiggling his thumb one more time.

Oh, John wants to go thumbin'. Quads use a thumb throttle.

"We could do that," I note. "But it's a weekday, so where can we go?"

"Oh, there are places. They aren't loggin' near Haslam today."

How does he know this? Who do you call to find out such things? Answer: John just knows.

Saltery Bay isn't that important.

John flashes his conquering smile. We're goin' thumbin'.

**W**e park in a hidden turnout just north of Duck Lake and off-load our quads. From there, we travel farther north along the eastern shore of Haslam Lake and across a logging bridge that is scheduled for removal. Large white "X" marks are painted on the metal base-boards of the bridge. We stop on the bridge so John can evaluate how he and his buddies will get across this creek once the bridge is gone. There is a mini-canyon below that looks insurmountable. But John says they can do it – it will just mean developing a trail farther upstream where the gully is not as steep.

"We could build the trail in a day. But they won't like us cross-ing the creek with our quads," says John. "It's watershed, you know. But take a look around you. See what they have done here, and somehow that's okay."

"They" are the logging company that has clear-cut this area near the lake. The hillside surrounding us on all sides has been rav-aged by recent logging. Pecker poles lie on the ground everywhere, the area denuded of cover. A few trees remain at the shoreline, but many of these will blow down now that the rest of the nearby forest is gone.

"Bastards!" says John. "They get away with this, and then we'll be told we shouldn't take our quads across the creek."

"Why is the bridge coming out?" I ask. It is obvious that the combination wood-metal bridge needs work, but I've seen far worse in this area.

"To keep us out, or so they think" accuses John. "They're done logging here, so they can get rid of the bridge." He sweeps his head around. "Then none of this is available to anybody. Of course, they can strip it as they see fit."

I know who "They" are.

\* \* \* \* \*

**A**s we proceed farther north, the dirt road is wet, recently sprayed, so that means there is logging activity today. But it isn't enough to worry John. I think about what I'd do if I come head-to-head with a logging truck screaming around one of the blind curves on this one-lane road. John has told me to head for the shoulder, and don't be afraid of the ravenous-looking ditch. It would be a rough exit.

There are some huge pieces of logging equipment – cranes and giant shovels – pulled off to the side of the road in occasional turnouts. All of these vehicles are idle for now. Logs stripped of their bark are piled on both sides of the road. The cut wood shines with a bright reddish-tan skin, providing a contrasting color to the surrounding blanket of forest green and dirt-gray.

The road becomes narrow, rocky, and rough. John slows in respect for Bro, who is bouncing around in his aft quad box. Bro shifts from side to side, trying to find a more comfortable riding position. There is no such position for a dog, but our quads have no problem with this terrain.

John comes to a halt, and I pull up behind him and stop. He is inspecting an area of fallen trees, stumps, and low brush to our left, near the head of Haslam Lake.

"They left our trail," he says, pointing to a narrow winding path that slides off the dirt road and snakes its way towards Haslam. "Usually they just doze it under."

John sounds almost thankful to "Them" for a change. Could these ogres actually be human? It's obvious that this trail has been consciously protected. Dirt and rocks are everywhere, except where this trail winds downhill from the road. It took a willful effort to save the trail in a normally brutal thrust of heavy logging equipment. There's hope.

\* \* \* \* \*

**A**t Giovanni Lake, we pause for lunch. Since my previous visit, the campsite area has changed so much I barely recognize it. At first, I assume we are at a different spot on the lake. But instead, ATV riders have simply reworked it. There is a new trail coming in, circumventing the former trail that is now cut off by logging activity. In the distance, you can hear the nearby drone of heavy equipment as another logging road is being built.

A new wooden bridge for quads terminates at the campsite, and a 50-foot dock now extends into the lake. Pokey has contributed a small rowboat to the site, and it sits upside down on a professionally-constructed wooden rack. In a small building that looks like a doghouse sits a cache of firewood. The only thing missing from this lush, remote campsite is people.

Giovanni's real name is "Giovanno," but locals often alter names in this area until recent tradition holds firm. Such is the case with the convolution of Giovanni Lake. How it happened in this instance is not clear. More understandable is the simplification of Frogpond Lake on Goat Island to Frog Pond or Olsen Lake to Olsen's Lake. Hammil Lake near Westview has been renamed locally as a more obvious landmark, West Lake.

Leaving the lake, we start back up the same trail. It leads to the logging road and will be a 20-minute battle with a rutted surface and a few significant water obstacles along the way. I'd call it a 5 on a scale of 1 to 10.

I lead the way out. This is a rare instance and maybe a bit dangerous. John constantly protects me by leading and keeping me in his rearview mirror. But for the first part of this trail, I need to be in front of him for some photos I want to shoot with John's quad approaching the camera. When I am done with the photos, I expect John to take back the lead.

"I'll pull over as soon as there is room, so you can pass," I offer.

"That's okay," says John. "Take it to the road. We can swap spots there."

The road is still 15 minutes away! I bounce ahead for some rarely-granted freedom in the lead. John always slows at each curve and checks his rearview mirror to make sure I am still behind him, but I don't need to take it slow today. John can take care of himself behind me, and he'll need to go slow through these ruts with Bro aboard. So I blast on ahead.

I know I'm not really on my own, but it feels that way in my imagination. I maneuver over the rough trail, using the skills John has taught me. Most of his instruction has been by the immersion method, an osmosis process that results from following behind John, tracing his track through the rough spots. Once in awhile, I wonder why he jogs to a particular side on a rutted corner, so I try the other side. I almost always notice that his less-than-obvious choice was the best, and I'm beginning to learn what goes into these decisions. This particular trail is a challenge in the solo mode, but I handle it well and am pleased with myself.

At first, I glance into my mirror to verify that John is still behind me (where else would he be?), but after a few minutes, I'm well out in front. There is only one route to the road (isn't there?), so why not get a dose of solo exploring?

Now and then, I concentrate to be sure there are no side trails that could split me from the established path, but it seems obvious this is the only route back to the road. Concentrating on side trails is easier said then done when you are busy analyzing the next set of ruts.

I burst out of the forest into a logging slash, and there's the road. I'm at least a few minutes ahead of John, so I back my bike off the road into a clear spot. Here I'll be out of the way of any logging traffic coming around the corner. I turn off my engine, remove my helmet, and prop my feet up on the front fenders. I wait for the sound of John's motor.

And I wait.

The mosquitoes start their relentless attack, as is always the case in June when you stop for more than a few minutes. And it's more than a few minutes. I glance at my watch – it's 2:25. I put my helmet back on and slide on my goggles to ward off the mosquitoes.

And I wait – 2:30, now 2:35. John's got problems. He should be here by now. Or maybe (yes, I've thought about this since pulling out onto the road), I'm on the wrong road. Could there have been a split in the trail that I missed? Is John waiting farther back on the road or even on another road? He'll really be pissed.

There's an engine. But it doesn't sound like a quad.

Around the corner comes a crummy, a bus-like truck used to carry loggers. Contrary to common opinion, this crummy is cruising slowly down the forest road, rather than hurtling out of control in the spirit of reckless crummy drivers. I wave nonchalantly, as if I sit engine-off along logging roads all the time.

The crummy's engine fades in the distance, and all is silent – 2:40. I'm getting worried. Could John have experienced mechanical problems? I never should have violated the keep-him-in-your-mirror rule. But with John? Who is more able to take care of himself than John?

Accidents do happen. Bikes break. Quads can turnover on rutted corners. But if I go back in, I'll meet John coming out, and it's hard to see around those corners. It's pretty much a one-way route. I'll wait until 2:45. That's now.

I crank up my quad and plunge back into the woods. Once I clear the slash, I slow and turn on my headlights. I look as far ahead as possible, and I'm also looking for trails jutting off on either side that I might have missed.

By the time I am about a mile into the woods, it is clear that something is drastically wrong. Even at John's reduced pace with Bro in his aft-box, I should have met him by now. I stop, turn off my engine, and await John's horn. He's done that before – waited for my engine to silence, and then provided a blast to let me know where he is. There is no horn. I wish I had a horn, and I consider yelling for John, but that seems futile. My voice would be attenuated within a few feet in this thick forest.

I stop every mile or so, turning off my engine and waiting. And at one stop, I can't get my bike into neutral so that I can restart it. The gearshift is locked in low, and it won't start in gear. I wrestle with the shift lever, rock the quad, push on the foot and hand brake, trying everything I know to get the bike into neutral. I get off the bike and try to rock it into gear. My heart is pounding. John is lying overturned in a ditch, and I am stuck. Time is wasting away fast. I hit the shift lever again, and it pops into neutral. A rush of relief speeds through me. There will be no more stopping. I've got to find John, and I've got to find him fast.

I'm on the downhill run, with the lake nearly in sight. I round one of the final curves, and there sits John on his quad. His bike is off to the side of the trail on a gravel road that juts off in a near-perpendicular angle to the trail. It's obvious. When John said "Take it to the road," this is the road he meant. How could I miss it? He's gonna be pissed.

But John is sitting on his bike patiently, looking like nothing has gone wrong. Nearly an hour has gone wrong.

I pull up beside him (wide, obvious road), cringe a bit, and turn off my engine.

"I knew you'd be back," comments John without expression. I know he is vexed, to say the least.

"I waited and waited at the road," I try to explain. "After awhile, I began to think something had gone wrong with you, even an accident." Maybe if I can refocus the problem, he'll sympathize with me a bit. I doubt it.

"Now do you know why I always keep you in my mirror?" he says.

"Yes, but I knew you could take care of yourself."

He still doesn't sound angry, almost apologetic. But this is an obvious road. How could I have missed it?

I try to distract him. That never works. "I kept stopping, turning off my bike to listen for your horn, and once I couldn't get it back into neutral to restart the engine."

"Oh, if that happens again, hold the rear brake, and you can start 'er in gear."

"That will work?" I ask. I think he told me about that before. The good news is that my distraction may be working.

"Yup, usually works."

There are a few moments of silence as I try to guess what will happen next. Maybe nothing.

Then John thrusts his hand downward beside his bike, pointing distinctly to the ground with a stern look. I know the message is coming, but I'm not sure what it is.

"For future reference, this…" He speaks slowly and pauses while still pointing downward at the gravel. "This is a road."

◇ ◇ ◇ ◇ ◇ ◇ ◇

# Chapter 4

## Goat

It is a few minutes after 8 AM when the sun rises through the mountain notch near the top of Goat Island during the heart of summer – sunrise delayed almost three hours by the foreground of the island's towering profile. First, the tall fir trees at the top of the ridge shimmer in a faint glow. Then they blaze brilliant white, with limbs clearly outlined. Suddenly, branches and trunks are silhouetted against the bright sky, reminding me of their true scale. The sun ruptures through the ridge, and moments later, the island-top trees return to their routine appearance, blending into the terrain – beautiful but no longer overwhelming in size, dwarfed by the brilliance of the sun.

I tend to think of this island as a mountain. It is a mountain that rises from the depths of the lake. It is a mountain that dominates my life.

When you look straight out the front door of my float cabin in Hole in the Wall, you're looking at Goat and the thoroughfare nearly everyone follows in this area of the lake. The only alternative is to swing all the way around Goat to the less-traveled east branch of the lake. Hole in the Wall is immediately north of First Narrows, and boat traffic up and down the Narrows is bounded by Goat. Only a few boats per day pass through here during the winter, and these vessels are primarily logging workboats and barges. During a weekend in the summer, recreational traffic increases considerably, although hours can pass even then without a single boat.

I stare perpetually at Goat and never grow tired of her unspoiled beauty. There are areas of the island that have been logged extensively, but the nub that I see is not part of that intrusion by man. The nearly vertical slopes rising from the lake in this area are beyond the capabilities of logging (except through use of helicopters). At present, the granite slopes just south of my Goat viewpoint are fully protected from logging by Crown law.

Steep waterfalls plunge down the side of the island-mountain. I hear them in the Hole's stillness during the winter and spring, but summer's dryness steals them from sight and sound.

On many days, low stratus clouds slide slowly through the Narrows, providing a swirling change of scenery, with Goat in the background. Sometimes these clouds are only scattered or broken (the prettiest portrait), and sometimes they are solid overcast. But as low as clouds come to the lake's surface, they seldom touch the water. Thus, fog is uncommon on this lake. There's often a low ceiling instead, 200 feet or less, with tops at about 400 feet, plastered right up against Goat. Under these conditions, the high ridges of the island are visible above the clouds, basking in the sunshine. This spectacular condition occurs quite regularly, enhanced by the constriction of moist air flowing through First Narrows. The resulting uplift in stable conditions is almost guaranteed to produce low stratus, even while the rest of the lake remains cloudless.

\* \* \* \* \*

One winter day, while I am on the backside of the float, a loud boom shakes the area. It sounds like a sonic boom (fighter jets from Comox sometimes use the lake for low-level navigation practice), but it doesn't quite fit that criteria. At first, I decide the boom is from loggers blasting a road in Chippewa Bay, but it is even louder than that and is clearly rumbling off Goat and the walls of First Narrows. In fact, the boom sounds like it is bellowing from Goat itself. When I walk around the cabin, smoke (dust) is mushrooming up directly across the Narrows where Goat meets the water.

The boom draws Margy from the cabin, and we meet at the front of the float. A landslide is still propelling rocks and debris into the lake. We watch a rising dust cloud and hear minor rumblings for a few more minutes.

We paddle over in the kayak as soon as we can launch from the float, and the damage is obvious. The boulders and trees roaring downslope have dragged the landscape with them, snapping several large trunks right near the shoreline. A particularly large tree is now completely underwater, stretched from the edge of the island until it finally disappears in deep water about 50 feet from shore.

The following summer, the path of devastation is still clearly evident, and the underwater tree becomes an obstacle for my fishing lures. I pass over the tree in my kayak, looking down on this artifact of the landslide.

The angle of repose of the Goat shoreline seems far steeper than possible for rocks and soil to retain their foundation. But somehow the trees and slope keep their position – most of the time. Evidence of an older landslide, just south of the one I observed, makes me wonder what it would have been like to be here for one of these massive slides. The plummet I witnessed provided a tremendous show of energy, but it was only miniscule compared to many of the previous landslides.

Loud booms in the Hole in the Wall are not uncommon. Excavation dynamite in Chippewa is the most common source, but one summer evening, thunderstorms (relatively rare here) push through the area. The echoes off Goat are tremendous, repeating themselves through reverberation off other nearby mountains. The rolling echo of a single clap of thunder can repeat itself at least four times here. When followed by another roll of thunder a few seconds later, the overlapping rumbling becomes even more impressive. It's a reminder that Goat is alive.

\* \* \* \* \*

During the winter, the sun rises nearly horizontally out of the south side of Goat Island at about 10 AM. It then arcs barely upward in a low path to the south, sinking into the trees just beyond John's Number 2 cabin before 3 PM. The light remains awhile longer, but the sun itself is visible less than five hours.

At all times of the year, where and when the sun rises with respect to Goat is a Druid-like computation. It's a reminder that the ancients tracked the seasons and relied on calendars based on terrestrial landmarks. In the early dark, as Christmas nears, I wait for the Pleiades to rise above a specific notch on Goat as 8 PM approaches. I know that notch, I know the Pleiades, and the season tells me when to expect the star cluster's first glimmer. It's reassuring to see the Seven Sisters reappear right on schedule

\* \* \* \* \*

There's something about Goat and rainbows. There's something, in general, about Powell Lake and rainbows, but the rainy reflections seem concentrated within the gravity of Goat Island.

Low sun angles in the west, accompanied by early evening showers, generate an abundance of rainbows. I chase them in my boat during the prolonged light of late summer afternoons, as I ride up the lake through sunshowers. Complete arcs and frequent double rainbows often stretch along the eastern shore.

I chase the pot of gold at the north end of a double rainbow past John's Number 1 cabin. The movement of the clouds to the west is perfectly timed as I progress northward, and the pot of gold passes abeam the Campion. I ride formation with it.

In boats, small rainbows are often self-produced by the rearward spray of water from the hull. Returning from the Head with John one summer evening, I try to relax in the back of the boat, although the waves are pounding us almost to my limit. I purposely focus on a mountain cap cloud near Beartooth to take my mind off my stomach. The boiling lenticular cloud churns as I inspect it. A lens-shaped swirl of white hovers over the peak, as I watch through the rough spray from the pounding hull. Sunlight catches the spray and spreads a small rainbow in front of Beartooth, in the foreground of the dazzling cap cloud.

* * * * *

**W**hen the stratus turns into low overcast, I listen for the sound of approaching motors. It's probably a boat, but often I'm treated to a floatplane flying along the logging work route between Shinglemill and the Head – up First Narrows, and right past the Hole. Under these conditions, the standard cruising altitude is 100 feet or less, and I mentally put myself in the cockpit, enjoying the ride. It might look dangerous from the outside, but from the inside it is the safest route available. The stratus bottoms are flat, and the lake's surface is as devoid of obstacles (only stray logs and boats!) as you can find anywhere.

* * * * *

$G$oat is more than an island. It is also more than a mountain. Another Goat is for fishing. Goat Lake, adjacent to Powell Lake, harbors large trout and is nearly devoid of people. There are few float cabins on Goat Lake, with Powell Lake the true float capital of Canada. The river connecting the two lakes is, of course, Goat River, and it is a challenging navigational exercise as you enter from the Powell Lake side. That is particularly true when the lake levels are low. First, you must carefully pick your way through the dead standing trees poking above the waterline. They mark the entrance to the river and are easily avoided, but it's best not to think too much about the snags below the water's surface at prop-strike depth. A slow speed and constant lookout are necessary. Gradually, you wind out of sight of both lakes until the river opens into mountain-edged Goat Lake. Continuing east, the first bay of Goat Lake constricts to an isolated vista. Usually, the water is dead calm in this part of the lake, even more placid than Hole in the Wall. More often than not, you have the entire lake to yourself.

Local campers and off-road ATV enthusiasts think of Goat as a road. Goat Main is one of the major forest service roads that winds through some of the most beautiful recreation spots in the world. You can drive this dirt road with a car (expect a bit of battle damage from flying rocks), but this route is most commonly traveled by quad, motorcycle, or truck. Goat Main, formally designated as Goat Lake Main, stretches north from Highway 101 near Lang Bay. It slides along the west shore of Lois Lake and then pushes nearly directly north along a recreational (and logging) chain of lakes. Finally, it reaches Goat Lake's south shore before veering farther northeast. The "Main" designation appropriately implies that there are endless tributaries for additional exploration. The logging roads and trails in this area seem endless.

But Goat Main wasn't built for fun. It was constructed for logging, and that's what it's reserved for during the week. It would be a nasty surprise to meet a logging truck coming around one of these curves. Logging trucks use their own VHF communication system ("Up the Main from Tin Hat") during the workweek. But these forest roads are open to the public on weekends, when they convert to recreational use.

＊ ＊ ＊ ＊ ＊

I think of Goat in all of these ways – an island, a mountain, a lake, a river, and a road. But primarily I think of Goat as a landmark. Once I sight Goat Island-Mountain, my geographic sense is properly oriented. Forming the central underpinning for Powell Lake, Goat sometimes seems the center of the universe. Gazing across the sparkling morning waters from my cabin in the Hole, Goat is the dominant power in my world.

◊ ◊ ◊ ◊ ◊ ◊

# Chapter 5

## Pruners of the Wilderness

When I arrive in Powell River the last day in May, the town is experiencing a heat wave, by Powell River standards. The entire previous week has been an early dose of summer, but this is the forecasted end of that anomaly.

I have my air conditioner set on "medium" (driver's window open in the ol' Ford Tempo) as I come down the hill from the airport. I always mentally gear-down rather quickly upon arrival – I sight the chuck and feel instantly acclimated. Today, as I approach the first (only) major intersection between the airport and John's house, there are two groups of teenagers crossing the street. All are wearing shorts, and one of the girls is celebrating with a bikini top. It isn't that warm, but Powell River tends to over-celebrate when summer finally arrives.

As I pull into the driveway, the house is a beehive of activity. Rick is lodged head-first in the rear seat of his taxi, a long power cord extending across the driveway. John's mom is on the sundeck above the garage and greets me with long, slow waves of both arms. John pulls his head out from under the hood of his old truck. His eyebrows are raised, as if he is surprised to see me. Sometimes he loses track of unimportant things, like dates on the calendar.

Bro attacks my car door immediately, coming from nowhere, pushing his head into my lap as I open the door. I rough up his ears, and he starts his madman dance designed for arriving visitors. As I walk up the driveway, he keeps bouncing off me.

"Hey, John! You didn't tell me it was already summer."

"Pretty hot, eh?" says John.

"Feels like 80," I reply. "Er, make that…25." It takes me only a few seconds to do the conversion to the C-scale. I'm getting better.

"80 might be a bit boiling for this place," says John.

Tools are scattered everywhere in front of the truck. Rick is out of his cab now, and I can see the cord leads to a vacuum cleaner, a wet vac.

"Working hard, as usual?" I yell to Rick.

"Oh, just cleaning up a bit," he replies. "Lots of droolers today."

"Droolers, eh?" (Is that really me with a BC "eh"? I've only been in town a few minutes.)

"They drool all over in there some days. It happens in this business."

John is already back under the hood. When he attacks a job, he doesn't let up until it's finished.

"What's broke now?" I ask.

"The heater," answers John. "It hasn't worked in weeks."

Most things don't work on John's truck most of the time. A dead heater seems like a minor inconvenience this time of year.

"Well, it's sure a nice hot day to get your heater in shape for next winter," I laugh.

"Yes, but it ain't working, and now it'll be fixed. You never know when you might need it," he retorts.

Can't argue with that.

\* \* \* \* \*

The false-summer gives way to rain nearly every day for the next two weeks. There is little accumulation of rainfall, but most days bring showers, and I need to light the fire in the stove almost every night in the cabin. It's certainly not like the Junes I remember in this area. I kid that this might be the year without a summer.

One Saturday, when we are scheduled for a quad ride, the morning dawns drizzly. I arrive at John's house at 9 AM, and it is obvious to both of us that a ride isn't going to work today, unless it's in John's truck. You can't get to the best places by truck, but the forest roads are open on weekends, and there's a lot to see. You just can't get to the same places as on a quad.

Rick was near Phelan Lake a few days ago, and he found an old trail just off Stillwater Main that leads toward the lake. He's convinced the trail can be followed on foot to the lake and then be improved for quad use. But he was by himself and without trail marking tape, so he wisely turned back when the trail started to blend into the forest. That's all John needs to hear. We have a rainy-day destination.

\* \* \* \* \*

We pull off Highway 101 and start up Goat Main. Within a mile, a doe and fawn appear in the middle of the road, and we grind to a stop to watch them. They bound down the road a little ways and then exit into the bush. While we're stopped, a powerful looking F350 pickup truck pulls up behind us and starts to pass. But they don't pass; instead they pull around and stop abreast of us in the road and roll down their passenger window. It's two of John's quad buddies, also out for a ride up the main on a day too rainy for quads. They saw a bear just a few hundred feet back, so we must have missed it by only a few seconds.

We talk (two pickups completely blocking the road) for at least 15 minutes about what replacement tires to buy for a Kodiak quad, how the fishing is in Lewis Lake, whether the upper road in Theodosia is going to be shut down, and about reports of landslides on the upper end of Goat Main. It's a good thing we are the only two trucks around, because the entire main is shut down in this spot while we bullshit. But no worries – for the entire remainder of the day, we won't see another human being on the logging roads until we exit back onto Highway 101.

Finally, we get moving again, letting the more powerful truck go first. It isn't that John's truck is a poor vehicle – it's just that it could be classified as a piece of junk. On the other hand, it always gets us where we want to go.

We continue up Goat Main and transition to Stillwater Main. As we approach Phelan Lake, it is beginning to rain hard. John stops momentarily just past a small bridge and asks me to look to my left to see if I can identify an old roadway that diverges into the forest. I can see a slight difference in the texture of the bushes, but it means little to me. John explains that nearly 20 years ago another main logging road, even bigger than the one we are on now, headed off to the left all the way to Dodd Lake. But the bridge over Freda Creek deteriorated and eventually came apart, and the road was deactivated. Now the forest has reclaimed the area, and it's almost impossible to see any signs of this major artery of the not-so-distant past. Nature works pretty fast around here.

Farther up Stillwater Main, we approach a wide dirt turnoff to our right, and John says this is near where Rick found the trailhead. As we park, the rain is still coming down pretty good, but we've come a long way to not at least try to find the trail.

We walk along the road, finding several spots that look promising, but pushing into the bush reveals dead ends in each case. Then John notices a few cut branches on the bushes. Rick is famous for snipping bushes that overhang trails with his heavy-duty clippers (pruning shears), and these clippings are pretty fresh. Who else would have been here lately?

Pushing farther into the bush in this area, the terrain slopes steeply downhill. John gets busy with his machete and I feign some help with my puny garden clippers. Bro bounces ahead of us and then returns to lend moral support, wagging his tail in a rhythm that fits between John's machete strokes (Oops, there goes my tail!).

Suddenly the bushes open into an obvious narrow trail that leads us rapidly downward toward Phelan Lake. Huge skunk cabbage and ferns are everywhere, interspersed with tightly-spaced trees, some of them large cedars.

"We can widen this for quads," says John. "Can't do it all by ourselves, but it can be done."

I look around and try to imagine how this small, rough footpath in dense timber can be widened and smoothed for vehicles of any size. But John says it is possible.

Fallen logs barricade the trail, but we can get around them. Bro is in the lead and seems to know exactly where he is going. I'm convinced he has an innate feel of the path of least resistance, and that is the definition for a trail of this type. Several times I think I've lost the trail, but then it reappears in front of me.

The rain is coming down now in huge drops. The forest canopy intercepts the falling rain, then delays it long enough for the drops to build in size by bumping into other drops. By the time the rain reaches the ground, it is a thick shower. I am getting soaked rapidly, my pants particularly receiving the brunt of the attack. And it is a cold rain. It reminds me of winter in this area. There are many days during the cold months that are warmer than this. But my jacket and boots are heavy enough to ward off most of the deluge.

John is tying bright pink trail marking tape at every obscure turn. We'll need it to retrace the trail in the future, and it may be required to get us out today. Because John is busy with the tape, I get to lead, a pleasure I seldom experience in our travels. I take full advantage of the opportunity to try to identify the trail's direction, and I do a pretty good job. Once in awhile, John has to call me back because I've made a wrong turn, but generally he lets me continue to track the trail, and I satisfy his standards.

"It's been a long time since anyone has been on this trail," he says. "Must be the cub scouts, or what they call junior forest wardens. You know, kids who learn to hike and explore."

"I can't imagine U.S. cub scouts tackling anything like this," I note. I can barely imagine me undertaking something like this.

Sure enough, some kind of organized group has been here. We step onto a huge log crossing a stream, and the log is covered with no-skid chicken wire. The closer we get to the lake, the more developed the trail seems to be.

The trail ends, after one more difficult stream crossing, in the delta of Freda Creek as it pours into Phelan Lake. It's almost beach-like with fine gravel and shallow water at the inlet. We pause for a few minutes here, but the rain isn't giving us any respite, so we start back up the trail.

The trail is easy to track as we climb upward from the lake, following the streamers of trail marking tape. We push out of the woods onto the road. I can hardly wait to get into the dry truck.

As soon as John enters the truck, he cranks the engine and turns on the heater – full blast. It seems the truck has been running only a few seconds, and already the recently repaired heater is pouring hot, wonderful air throughout the cab.

"Feels mighty good," I proclaim.

"Like I said, you never know when you might need it, do you?"

A heater standing by in the cold and wet of summer is not a bad idea, after all.

\* \* \* \* \*

The next day, summer has returned. Or so we hope. Vancouver Island to the west is bathed in sunshine, and it seems logical that the clearing is moving our way. But the forecast is not promising.

It is winter-cold as we rattle up the main from Lois Lake. The sign says: "Starting Up Goat Main Loop," not a tourist notice but a VHF radio reporting point for logging trucks. This is a rare spot where a "loop" provides one-way travel on a logging road.

John and Rick are in front, riding side-by-side, taking advantage of the one-way travel. Riding abreast eliminates the dust-distance. Trucks won't be encountered as they roar down the main (probably). Dave follows a dust-length behind, with Jayne doubling on his quad. Dave and Jayne ride a loose formation with me. Rob, John's third brother, may be joining us at Murphy Lake.

As we cruise up the main, the clouds are threatening. If precipitation begins, it might be snow – in June, no less!

By the time we reach the Murphy Lake turnoff, rain has begun. It is light, cold, and persistent. The trail is narrow but barely wide enough for Rick to pull up next to John, reach over and pat Bro on the head, and have a discussion with his brother. They continue to ride side-by-side for a few minutes as they drive slowly and discuss the situation. John points to the left, and Rick nods as they continues to survey the forest to the left side of the trail as we climb higher. They're looking for something.

Now they slow even further and then stop. I pull up behind them, and John turns to explain:

"If it gets any worse, we can get out of the rain in there."

The brush and forest look thick here, but it doesn't look like a pleasant place to escape the rain.

"Do you see it?" asks John.

There is something else besides the forest here, but I don't see it. Wait, there's something brown. It's an old wooden structure.

"A cabin!" I say.

"It's been abandoned a long time," explains John.

"Do you think they have TV?" I joke.

"Probably not," replies John.

We press on up the trail, and within less than a half-mile it starts to pour. Four quads turning around on a narrow trail is not easy, but it can be done when you want to get dry.

By the time we return to the cabin, we find that the forest cover alone is thick enough to keep us pretty dry. That's good news, since the inside of the cabin is trashed. Broken furniture is piled within the structure, and I imagine all kinds of animals bored into the dirt floor. But this is a good lunch stop, and by the time we are ready to move on, the rain has stopped.

On the remainder of the climb to Murphy Lake, increasingly deeper trenches challenge us. The last two are mini-canyons, with considerable running water, boulders, and logs that have been washed down the creeks. I've been here before on my 100cc motor-cycle, and I didn't make it through. I wiped out twice in the first mini-canyon, and John had to double-back and ride my motorcycle through – without difficulty, of course. On a quad, this is challenging but relatively easy. We truck on through and stop at the rounded-out parking area in the bushes above Murphy Lake.

It's a short but steep hike down to the lake, but today it will be more physically demanding than that. There is a recently-added trail for hikers and bikers, and John and his brothers plan to groom it for an easier descent to the lake. Sounds simple.

The process is not as orderly as I imagined. Trails have been constructed all over the region, but I envisioned it as a project that occurs slowly in a variety of steps that begins with a rather scientific survey of the terrain and eventually ends with preening the trail. In reality, all of the steps occur rather simultaneously.

Rick, Dave, and Jayne start at the top, whacking through the brush with their clippers to find the path that is already nearly re-claimed by nature. They toss aside dead logs that block the path and closely clip the branches that border the overgrown trail, snipping close to the trunk to prevent danger to riders. It's a process that simultaneously prepares a path and improves the health of the forest. You might call it pruning the wilderness.

While Rick, Dave, and Jayne whack at things at the top, John and I hike downward to survey the terrain to determine the route. We do some minor clipping as we proceed, but we end up clearing several false paths that are dead ends. Routes that look fine to me have bedrock obstacles that worry John and switchbacks that have inadequate corner clearance. He is worried less about slope and more about maneuvering room. I view things with an eye on avoid-ing the most grunt work, and John looks at things from aspects of the general flow of the terrain.

We finally find a route that won't get us all the way to the lake to-day, but it should provide refurbishment of the original path. Later, we can return with heavier tools.

I remember my previous visit to this spot a year ago. Hiking down to the lake was challenging. Hiking back up was a significant climb. Today, I walk up and down these slopes in segments at least a dozen times. This is major labor.

At first, it seems hopeless. The route is far from obvious, and our progress on clearing the trail seems miniscule. It appears we will make only a dent in things today. Yet, by the end of the day, the quad trail is basically complete over halfway to the lake. This happens by prying rock obstacles loose, cutting fallen logs, clipping branches, clearing brush, and moving a lot of dirt. Fallen logs are moved to the edge of the steepest turns to allow buildup of a safety edging and the prevention of further erosion.

Dave takes rock excavation seriously. He attacks some deep-seated boulders that look like they are bedrock. Some are impossible to move, but you don't know until you dig around them. If a boulder can't be moved, the trail must deviate around it to prevent damage to the undercarriage of quads. Running water has rutted the slope and makes rocks protrude within the trail. The digging and sweating go on continuously for hours, and all of sudden, you can see the refurbished flow of the trail. It has progressed from an impossible forested cliff to a developed trail that winds down toward the lake.

Of course, it has to be tested. Rick is, appropriately, the first to drop down the initial steep entry point on his Kodiak. We wonder if we'll have to winch him out. By the end of the day, all quads except mine are using the upper portion of the new trail, and Dave has thrashed with his quad down to a point about a third of the way to the lake. It takes all of us to get him turned around and out. I'm wise enough to declare my amateur status and keep my bike topside.

Just as we start to run out of steam, John hears bikes approaching.

"Listen," says John. "Quads. Must be Pokey."

I hear nothing, but minutes later the buzz of the four-stroke engines are faintly evident.

Pokey and Babe park their bikes above the new trail and walk down to join us. (How does John hear quads so far away? Better question: How does he know it is Pokey?)

Babe is a brute of a guy. I immediately analyze his physique and figure he is either a lumberjack or a prizefighter. Although he is no spring chicken, he jumps in with a tree limb for a crow bar and starts moving huge boulders and ripping at errant decayed roots that are as big as he is. His energy is extraordinary, and we feel puny beside him.

"New muscles," says John. "Ours are giving out today." Babe raises an excavated boulder over his head and tosses it 10 feet. It shakes the ground under my feet when it reaches earth.

Pokey is pushing hard too, although his cardiologist would have a fit. Their wives have doubled in with them, and they are slipping down the improvised trail to the lake. There's lots of dirt flinging every which way, and the job site is in full swing, with new muscles picking up where the old ones are starting to slow down.

Rob shows up an hour later, when most of the work is done (well timed). I am amazed to learn he has driven his pickup truck most of the way on the Murphy Lake trail. He finally had to stop at one of the last mini-canyons and hike the rest of the way. (I later watch him slowly extract his truck from the forest – he must have a mighty strong oil pan.)

Accompanying Rob are Karen and their new Shih Tzu, a yiping tiny white monster with a face covered with hair. It's a category that John calls "kick dogs." John, Bro, and Shih Tzus don't mix well.

Rob's arrival is a great excuse to close out the work for the day, so we hike the rest of the way to the lake and pause for a second lunch. Rob and I are more interested in fishing than eating, so we launch the raft that is tied to a log and take advantage of the plentiful native trout. The fish are small but feisty and fun to catch and pull aboard the raft on our barbless hooks. None are keepers.

The day has turned out to be more work than expected. I'm just a tourist, following John and trying to stay out of trouble. As is typical, when the ride begins, I wonder why I am putting such effort into flogging myself continually in rugged terrain on a quad. But now I am floating on a raft on Murphy Lake. In all directions, there are snow-patched peaks with waterfalls roaring down rocky cliffs, spilling from mountains with no names. To the east, McVey Lake is hidden from view behind a wall of granite, with waterfalls directing the outlet creek downward into Murphy Lake. Soon, if I'm lucky, John will take me there, another spot that is too beautiful and challenging to imagine.

# Chapter 6

## Dark Nights

G oat is my front porch, day and night. It forms a familiar backdrop for my evenings as an amateur astronomer.

From a darkness standpoint, my first nights as a new cabin owner are disappointing. I arise in the middle of the night, fumble for my flashlight, and climb down from the loft. When I step outside, the lack of darkness disheartens me. Cloudy skies produce brighter nights, and these first cloudy nights seem as bright as those at home in California. A nearly full moon adds to the effect. The clouds are so thick that the moon's location is barely apparent; I can tell it is somewhere to the south. This disappointment lasts for nearly a week, but the weather forecast finally calls for clearing skies, and the moon is now waning past last quarter and will not affect the sky until nearly dawn.

I completely miss the first clear night. I sleep through it. The next morning, Margy tells me how she arose in the night, stepped out on the deck, and was overwhelmed by the stars. She also provides an example of how dark it is on the deck, how the bright stars are reflected in the calm water.

I'm not going to miss the stars again. I set my alarm for 2 AM. But I am awake before the alarm, just after midnight. The window above my head confirms the stars are burning bright. If they are this bright through the glass, what awaits me on the deck? Down the stairs, fumble with the door (the screen sometimes jams a bit as the float sways and the cedar foundation twists in response), and out onto the deck. The stars bombard me with a brilliance I can only remember once before when camping near Port Hardy. I look for Polaris as orientation. The Little Dipper hangs upside down, with only its bowl visible above the cliff. Polaris and the Big Dipper are below the treeline and the rock wall to the north, but the Little Dipper still identifies true north, and now everything else falls quickly into place. One corner of the Summer Triangle (Deneb) is perched directly overhead, with bright Vega dominating the sky to the west and Altair the southwest. The constellation of Cygnus (the Northern Cross) stretches above me, with the Milky Way winding bright across the center of the sky. An amateur astronomer (that's me!) is looking at heaven.

I once had the opportunity to spend a night at the eyepiece of the 60-inch telescope on top of Mount Wilson in southern California. My amateur astronomy club rented the telescope and its operator for the entire night. Jupiter was so bright in the eyepiece that you could only keep your eye in place for a few seconds. (Later, a planetary filter was added to the eyepiece, but the initial blast of light had a memorable effect.) Yet, outside the observatory dome, the Milky Way was not even visible. Except on the very darkest nights on Mount Wilson, with near-perfect seeing conditions in stable air, the lights of Los Angeles prohibit the viewing of the Milky Way. What a sad historic state for one of the most famous observatories in the world.

On my float deck, I stand transfixed by the night sky, my neck craned back – and now aching. I perform a quick test of astronomical seeing and transparency, easily noting the Andromeda Galaxy as a fuzzy dot. The Little Dipper is an excellent test of both personal vision and atmospheric conditions, and I can see every basic star in the bowl plus a few strays that are in unfamiliar positions. I am seeing stars approaching sixth magnitude, no small feat for my marginal eyes.

My focus now turns to the landscape around me. It is not totally dark. To the south, the glow of Powell River is evident, and I can easily see Goat Island across the water, silhouetted starkly against the stars to the east.

Directly off the front of the deck, two floating pond lights glow bright green. These solar-powered lights are tethered to the log breakwater – reassuring reminders of civilization in the dark. Tonight, in contrast to the surrounding darkness, the pond lights blaze exceedingly brilliant. Nearby float cabins are not discernible, but…

What's this? Lights on the water everywhere. How can this be? Flickering lights on the water sparkle in a gentle breeze that ruffles the surface. At first, I remember the ocean glow that I have seen in Hawaii. In the bright illumination of Honolulu's shoreline hotels, lights ride the crests of breaking waves near the beach. The tops of the waves glow wonderfully radiant, a spooky sight until it was explained to me that this is the common glow from bioluminescent ocean plankton. That is what I am looking at now.

Bioluminescent plankton in Powell Lake? No, this glow is different. These are distinct lights, not at all diffuse. Then I remember what Margy reported from the previous night – how could I have forgotten? These are stars in the water, reflected from the constellations above. And it is not only bright Vega and Deneb. Points of light shine everywhere in the water. I look closer and recognize the entire constellation of Lyra (composed of rather dim stars, except for Vega). Lyra shimmers as a strangely inverted image in the water.

* * * * *

My 7 X 50 binoculars are among the best astronomical instruments under a dark sky. The wide field of view (50 millimeter lenses) makes them ideal for light gathering. My 7 X 50s have followed me through life. They were my first serious astronomical tool as a teenager, and they get more exercise today than ever before.

The exceptional astronomical seeing conditions in the Hole provide vivid contrast between deep sky objects and the dark sky. Some of these objects span fields of view wider than the moon, so excessive telescopic magnification obliterates their grandeur. Even with a low power eyepiece, a telescope can't capture the full spread of the Andromeda Galaxy. My binoculars serve as light buckets for the deep sky.

It doesn't take long to recognize that I have a unique opportunity to harness my love of astronomy to the ideal observing conditions of the Hole in the Wall – except, of course, for the movement of the float. That motion is not a problem for seven-power binocular magnification, but I expect it to be a challenge for a telescope. My trek toward a precision amateur telescope on the float will be an interesting journey. But even before that excursion begins, binoculars and my naked eyes serve my initial needs.

In recent years, I've developed an intense desire to return to my roots in astronomy, and this float is the perfect place. As a fallback position, a bedrock telescope mount would be possible on the adjacent shore. (It will prove unnecessary.)

I have ogled computerized Go-To telescopes for years. Go-To equipment allows the observer to automatically slue a telescope to precise stellar coordinates, a quantum leap from the basic astronomical instruments of my youth.

Several years ago, during a visit to the outskirts of Tucson, I spent a night at a semi-professional observatory that doubles as a bed-and-breakfast. In an effort to bring astronomy to the public, a 16-inch reflector in a small observatory is adjoined to a sliding-roof observing deck with several small Go-To telescopes. Arizona tourists with an interest in astronomy pay for lodging that is accompanied by views through the small telescopes and a quick peek through the larger, semi-professional 16-inch reflector.

Cleo (short for Cleopatra) is the bed-and-breakfast hostess and receptionist for the observatory. Upon my arrival, she provides the standard tour of the facilities. As Cleo explains the procedures for use of the telescopes and associated library materials, she throws out a few astronomical tidbits. Many of these factoids are precise, and I recognize their accuracy because of my strong background in astronomy. I assume from Cleo's confident presentation that she is an astronomer of serious amateur pedigree. But her presentation seems a bit stilted, almost rehearsed. We pause before a wall photo of the Andromeda Galaxy, and Cleo explains some facts. This is the 31st object in Messier's catalog of nebula, and thus carries the designation of M31. It is very large and a long way from earth – over a million miles. A million miles? Not quite. How about three million light-years (not miles)? Maybe it is just a slip of the tongue.

As Cleo continues the tour, I soon realize that she has learned some basic astronomical facts and can apply them to her job as hostess. It doesn't take much to sound like an expert in any field.

Cleo explains that this particular month is unique, since a blue moon will appear later in the week. She can't wait to see the blue tint of the moon. (Blue moons indicate rare months with two full moons; there is no blue tint, and the event is of no interest to astronomers.) Then she explains the arrangements for the evening, which include the optional "rental" of a local astronomer. I immediately decide to take advantage of that tantalizing extra, and our University of Arizona graduate student shows up soon after sunset to guide me through the skies with a small Go-To telescope.

The computerized scope is all that I expect it to be. The simplicity of the computer interface allows the operator to drive the telescope to any distant object (Go-To M31). Having used manual equatorial drives for years, the ease of use of a computerized scope blows me away. And the optics are exceptional for such a small instrument. I want one of these telescopes. But how can the light polluted skies of southern California justify such a purchase decision?

As my rented student astronomer jumps from object to object, I notice Cleo nearby, assisting another astronomical tourist. She cranks up a Go-To telescope and starts pushing the buttons. The telescope slues flawlessly to each object on her observing list. As a novice, Cleo uses the Go-To features to lock onto objects that I have never been able to find with my older equipment. At one point, it is apparent that the astro-tourists are looking at M31, for I hear Cleo say: "And it's hard to believe, but this galaxy is over a million miles away."

Several years later, my first Go-To telescope comes out of its factory box in California. Within days, it is en route to the dark skies of Hole in the Wall.

M31, the Andromeda Galaxy, with satellite galaxy M110 below it.

# Chapter 7

## Four

In a light rain at the gas station, we top off our quads with marine fuel. The previous evening's forecast included occasional drizzle during the night. It poured hard and nearly continuously since about 10 PM, but has finally let up.

John's 660cc Grizzly is in the bed of his truck, with the trailer behind holding my 420cc Kodiak and Margy's 230cc Honda. John is tempted to sneak some marine fuel into his truck, but the local gas stations are getting more concerned these days. I try to convince him it is okay, but he doesn't budge. That's probably for the best, since I constantly wonder if someone is going to deport me. If they do, it'll probably be for something more important than pumping a few gallons of cheap marine gas into a pickup truck.

Alex and Toni pull up in their truck in the gas aisle next to us. I don't know them, but they are John's neighbors, and they have a new Special Edition silver Grizzly in the bed of their truck. And they are going on one of their first quad rides. They've been looking for John this morning, and now they've found him.

From such a description, you know this is a small town. Here are John's neighbors (not down the street – right next door), and they have a Grizzly like John's. They want John to lead them on one of their first indoctrination rides, and here we all are at a gas station. When you're from Los Angeles, it's almost spooky.

It's Boxing Day, the day after Christmas that even Canadians don't seem to understand. It's a major holiday, the logging roads are open to us, and everyone is headed for Freda Creek. Why all local ATV enthusiasts go to Freda Creek on Boxing Day is buried somewhere in tradition. I've been to Freda, but not on Boxing Day, and it's hard to imagine everyone sitting around chewing the fat in the cold. I suppose the brave venture into the creek with their quads for a few minutes, and I bet there are a lot of electric winches standing by, hoping for some action.

Fortunately, John wants to go somewhere else, preferably a long way from Freda Creek. We leave town on the road south of Haslam Lake, but it is a washboard from the recent rains. With the quad trailer behind us, it's a rough ride, so John elects to park quickly, rather than bounce up and down all the way to Duck Lake. The spot he picks to pull off the road is on a significant slope. In fact, the bed of his truck is contorted into a laterally twisted condition at the edge of the road. It's an old truck, but I didn't know it could bend like this.

Alex and Toni are doubling on their Grizzly, and they offload quickly. It takes us awhile to get organized, with three quads to unload. The good news is the rain has stopped. But John isn't expecting cooperation from the weather, so he changes into his rain gear and explains to a resistant Bro that his doggie raincoat will be needed today. Bro reluctantly accepts his blue velcro jacket with a muted whine.

After the two quads on our trailer are off, John decides to save some time by not disconnecting the trailer from the truck. Instead, he backs his quad from the truck to the trailer, and then from the trailer to the ground. It would have been even faster with two sets of ramps, as Margy and I scurry to move the ramps rearward in the strange but efficient process. John is a hard worker when he works, but he also takes pride in working hard to avoid work.

Alex and Toni have already left – they'll wait for us at the Duck Lake intersection. John departs behind them, while Margy and I are still fumbling with our equipment. It's a damp day, and Margy complains that her goggles fog as soon as she puts them on.

"Try this," I say, pushing my goggles up above the visor on my helmet. "Pull them down once we get rolling, when there's some airflow." I feel like a quad scientist. But Margy elects to stow her goggles in her aft carrying case. Finally, we're ready to ride.

Margy leads and I follow her up the dirt road. Around the first corner, just past the gravel pit, I hear a loud horn, and look into my rearview mirror. There's John. It's one of his favorite tricks. He gets behind me by lying in-wait at the gravel pit turnoff.

John passes me, and a few miles later we are approaching the Duck Lake intersection. I remember my goggles, and reach up to pull them down. They're gone. Somewhere between the truck and here, they popped off the top of my helmet. I'm no longer a quad scientist.

As we pull into the turnout near Duck Lake, I'm not sure what to do. I should confess about my goggles and return to find them. They're expensive. Plus, I don't want to go on without them. But at least a dozen quads are sitting in the turnout, and these are riders from the ATV Club. You hate to admit you are stupid in front of others. It's easier in private.

I confess to John that I lost my goggles, and his instructions are not unexpected: "Go back and get 'em" is his simple recommendation. It sounds a lot more like an order than a suggestion.

So I turn around and hustle back towards the truck, checking the sides of the road as I speed along. A group of four quads pass in the opposite direction as I continue along the road. Surely they would have seen my goggles, if they were lying in the road. Riders don't miss bright red objects, and they would pick them up. I should have flagged the riders down and asked if they found my goggles, but now it's too late. I'm on a mission to waste more time, and John ain't gonna like it.

I look along the road's edge, since the goggles couldn't be near the road's center. Otherwise, the riders I just passed surely would have picked them up. I'm concentrating intently, when John's truck finally appears around the bend. And there, right in the center of the road opposite the truck, are my red goggles. How could those riders have missed them?

Now it's a big rush at 60 klicks to get back to the turnout. By the time I get there, all of the quads except our small group have departed for Freda Creek. As we regroup near Duck Lake, John gives me the evil eye, although he's glad I recovered my goggles. He hates inefficiency.

With our engines temporarily silenced, we can hear the faint roar of quads north of us. There is a giant mass of ATVs and 4X4 trucks converging on Freda Creek, but it's not going to include us.

"It's a good day to keep off the main," says John. I'm grateful that's his attitude.

\* \* \* \* \*

**A**s we climb the increasingly challenging grade to Granite Lake, snow begins to appear along the side of the trail. Then it emerges in scattered clumps on the trail itself. Within another half mile, the entire landscape is white. Several trenches, with puddles not yet frozen, greet us. But the climb is uneventful except for the serenity the snow brings. It's not deep enough to challenge our quads. In fact, it seems to soften the road below us and brings a sense of warmth rather than cold. It's nice to be wrapped in our cold-weather gear.

As the snow-cover increases, the bushes along the side of the narrowing trail become obstacles as they overhang our path under their burden of snow. John, as the leader of the pack, stops to whack the bushes, relieving them of their load so they can spring skyward and away from the trail, allowing us to pass without hindrance. When the branches pop upward, John ducks to avoid the plummet of snow. Bro is not as lucky, and a major downfall of white powder crashes over his aft quad box. A few seconds later, Bro's blue raincoat reappears from the white avalanche. The black Lab looks disgusted and more than a little humiliated.

At the turnout for the final drop down to the lake, John stops and suggests that Margy not try this. Her quad is not four-wheel drive, and he expects the slope to be slippery, but he thinks I can make it fine on my bike. Margy doubles on my quad, and down we go.

It's not as tough as I expect, and within minutes we are in the turnout area at Granite Lake. The landscape is a picture postcard. I walk back up the path a short ways and photograph the lake and the quad parking area. It's a winter wonderland, not too cold but thoroughly covered by snow. The lake is frozen, but the ice is far too thin to venture onto.

John would like to take us farther up the trail that leads above Granite Lake. He and Rick have been working hard on reopening the trail that was originally a logging road. But in this snow, there would be little possibility we could make the climb. It will have to wait for another season.

"It's beginning to snow," says Margy excitedly. We don't get snow in Los Angeles.

"Not good," says John. "Guess what's going on down below?" John hates rain.

Sure enough, a pleasant snowy interlude above turns into frigid rain below. In fact, by the time we reach the logging road and begin our trek back to the truck, it is pouring. Everyone is thoroughly soaked, John and Bro less extensively because of their rain gear. They seem to detest the rain, while we absorb the wet and cold as a small price to pay for a visit to a beautiful winter lake. Of course, it doesn't rain much in Los Angeles either.

The ride seems longer going back to the truck, and we're all glad to get out of the rain when the quads are finally loaded. It's a crowded truck seat, with Bro and three wet humans. Bro is totally disgusted with the weather. In fact, he does something I've never seen him do before. Normally, he piles into the truck after a quad ride and immediately plops down in the center of the seat, demanding at least as much room as two people. Today, he turns around and faces rearward. He just sits there, as if he is turning his back on both the weather and us

As we pile into the truck, Margy whines about wanting electric heaters for her handgrips and thumb-throttle before the next winter season. All the way back to town, Bro rides ass-end to the front, totally disgusted.

\* \* \* \* \*

On a cloudy June day, John and I start up the trail to Granite Lake again. The first major trench is more challenging than I remember from the previous winter. As we progress farther, my mind attempts to compare this often granite-sloped path with the smoother trail of winter. Maybe it is the lack of snow to cushion the ride that makes this trail seem so different today, or maybe it is how my mind works. In any case, it's a challenging climb, with John stopping momentarily to point to a family of baby grouse under the bushes adjoining the edge of the trail. Only a few hundred feet later, a large, adult grouse takes awkward flight to our left, flopping away ungracefully rather than truly flying.

As we approach the lake, we make the turnoff and descend into the same parking spot as the previous December. This time the final drop to the lake is extremely simple. In fact, if it were not for the memory of December, it would be a total non-event. So here rests the mystery of one's mind. Most of the trail today seems more challenging than in the snow, but the most challenging section from winter memories is now merely a whisper. Maybe snow does that to quads, and maybe minds are a mysterious thing. Probably both.

"The trout are almost-black here," says John, as I pull off my helmet. "Give it a try. The lake is pretty much fished out, but they seem to be coming back."

"On my first cast, I nab an 8-inch trout, and he flops off my barbless hook within a few feet of shore. A few casts later, I land another small trout. John is right – the fish is almost pure black, a very strange looking creature.

"Is it a cutthroat?" I ask, holding it out for both of us to inspect. (Bro too – he's leaping frantically trying to get a bite.)

"I'd say it's a rainbow," replies John. "You can't see the normal red throat marking of cutthroat, although it could be hidden by the black. The side markings are those of a rainbow."

Trout, a universally beautiful fish, are disturbingly ugly when they are charcoal black. I hand the pole to John. While he fishes, I snap a few photos from the same location I shot the winter photo. It is quite a comparison of landscape. It's the exact same geographic location – different season, totally different "place."

While I am taking the photos, John hooks a slightly bigger black trout. The other black one (Bro) impatiently awaits the landing of the catch. John extracts the trout from the lake successfully, but faces a challenge in returning it to the water. Bro stands ready (as always) as John tries to revive the fish in the shallow water before releasing it. The trout springs to life quickly, flaps its tail fin, and Bro pushes his nose into the water at the release site.

"No!" says John firmly. His admonition is a waste of effort with Bro, as the dog awaits the freeing of the fish from John's hands. But fish outwits dog. At first, as John releases the trout, it swims slowly, then tauntingly whips towards Bro and is gone in a flash. Bro is miffed. You can tell by his "I'm disgusted" snort.

Back on the trail, we slow to cross a wooden bridge at Granite Lake's inlet stream. It's a bridge groomed with care by John's friends – a solid structure that barely vibrates as we cross.

The trail steepens and narrows, with scattered trenches and muddy ruts. We pass a carved sign pointing toward Elk Lake. Would anyone come this far without knowing exactly where they are going?

John pulls to a stop and shuts off his engine.

"I need to fix this," he says, as he extracts his chainsaw from his bike's front box. Years ago, alders reclaimed this logging trail, as they often do as soon as a road is abandoned. The small trunks have been cut to near-ground level, but now the runoff has dug around the roots, projecting the narrow stumps upward into unacceptable clearance for our quads. The dead roots haven't grown, but the ground has receded around them.

The alder stumps are in clumps, projecting out at odd angles. When you hit them with one of your low-pressure quad tires, it's amazing there isn't a puncture every time. The four-psi inflation, coupled with thick rubber, provides superb durability and a relatively soft ride, considering the terrain. Quads ride over sharp obstacles, including rough rocks, amazingly well. Eventually, you can loose a tire, especially if you whack a sidewall on a sharp root like these.

John gives his chainsaw's starter rope a quick snap. It starts on the first pull.

"Alder seeds sprout in these old roads," notes John. "Snow-load keeps them stunted. So the trunks spread out in all directions. Makes a mess."

John buzzes through a few of the denser clumps with his saw, and I clear the residue wood from the trail behind his strokes. It's impossible to tackle all of the stumps, but this area is now more passable.

In another half-mile, now well past the Elk Lake turnoff, we arrive at the base of a steep incline. John stops, stands on his footrests, and swivels his torso around to face me. I pull up close behind to get the message.

He raises his left hand high, with four fingers extended. Four what?

I shrug my shoulders and squint at John with an expression of "What?" Even through my helmet and goggles, I bet his eagle eyes can see the lack of understanding on my face.

John pumps his left arm, with four fingers still extended and shoved toward me. From my vantage point, he is thrusting his fingers at me.

I shrug again. Then it hits me.

"Oh, four!" I shout over the noise of our engines. He probably can't hear me but probably can read my lips. And he obviously sees my right thumb move down and hit the four-wheel-drive button. John nods in satisfaction, turns back to the trail at hand, and starts upward. Four.

It's quite a climb. Bro bounces from side to side in his rear quad box, checking out the scenery and holding on for dear life. John stops at a flat spot, just before a wide turn.

"Take a look over there." He points to an area of brush off the side of the road. When I look closer, I see alders leading into the rugged forest.

"That's where the original logging road ran," notes John. "We couldn't get through when we tried to reactivate the road. It's a real mess."

"It must have been tough making a new trail segment here," I reply.

"Not just tough, but supertough," says John. "In fact, take a look up there." John points to the rising terrain off our right side. "We weren't sure how to get through this segment, so Rick, Dan, and I started off separately on three different routes. That's the direction Rick tried, and Dan went that way." His arm sweeps over the broad almost-cliff farther to the right.

After starting three separate trails simultaneously, they finally came to consensus. The three riders regrouped on the segment John started, and together they made it far enough to join the old overgrown logging road.

"I call this stretch '10,000 Alders', but it doesn't really have a name," says John. He has his own names for nearly everything.

We're headed to the end of the trail now, a nearly flat stretch of granite and soft dirt that John calls "Blue Ridge" and a turnaround at the end he's named "Quad Lookout." The view at the point is unbelievable.

It's a cloudy, hazy day. I can only imagine what this would look like on a clear day, with puffy cumulus in the foreground of a bright blue sky. There's a light wind, warding off the mosquitoes.

In every direction forest mixes with water. Even in the haze, I look south and see the Thormanby Islands and Welcome Passage, well past Pender Harbour and the tip of Texada. To the west, Savary and Hernando Islands are easily identified. So is Campbell River, all the way across the Strait of Georgia.

On the northern side of our perch, Haslam Lake spreads out far below us, and in any direction, several lakes are visible simultaneously. Elk, March, and Dodd Lakes dominate to the north, with many interspersed smaller ponds.

"That one doesn't have a name," says John pointing at a clearing with a mirror-like lake. "Neither does that one, but I've been there."

Glaciated peaks cover the northern skyline. To the northeast is majestic Mount Alfred. More easterly, the Knuckleheads jut upward in all of their splendor. Lakes, mountains, forest, and the ocean cover 360 degrees. It's a sweep of a supernatural region seldom seen by tourists. I thank my lucky stars (and John) for bringing me here. Of course, four-wheel drive helps.

◊ ◊ ◊ ◊ ◊ ◊

# Chapter 8

# Barbless Hooks

If there was ever a lake that looks like trout, this is it. Stories abound about the giant trout hauled from Powell Lake, but that is mostly in the past. For reasons that don't seem logical (rationale differs from expert to expert), giant trout are rarely caught in Powell Lake these days, but smaller trout are in abundance. Of course, smaller still means bigger trout than I've caught anywhere else.

I enjoy fishing, but have strayed from it in recent decades. Probably my biggest deterrent to even trying was lack of success in catching even the smallest fish most of the time. On Powell Lake, that all changed. If you're willing to settle for 10-inch trout, they're plentiful. Most summer evenings, you can see them jumping just outside the breakwater logs. Often they tempt you by their splashes inside the logs, in front of the picnic table or in the adjacent swimming hole. Most of this splashing activity is in the late evening. In the summer, evening means 10 PM or later, as the sun dips below the northwestern horizon only to reappear in the northeast seven hours later. One evening at about 10 PM I caught a 10-inch cutthroat directly off my front deck, inside the breakwater – right off my front porch.

My fishing poles remain on the deck continually, and a favorite misuse of my time is to stop whatever I'm doing (particularly near sunset) and throw a few casts at strategic points around the float. Trout love to hang out near and under logs. The float and breakwater make a nifty home for them. The human activity on the float is not a particular incentive for the fish, but throwing a line from your house is a relaxing pursuit for a fisherman, so I regularly make a circuit of the cabin with a few casts. Trout love to hover under my docked boat, so that area always gets my attention.

One June evening, I am conducting my typical around-cabin circuit at sunset. The water is perfectly calm, and I get a solid strike off the front porch, but the fish is only on my line a few seconds. I hop aboard the Campion (tied to the float) to cast closer to the log breakwater, and then I work my way behind the cabin and out the new dock finger. This floating extension was constructed by John to provide more docking space, and it provides a nice expansion of my fishing territory. Usually the tin boat is docked on the outside of this finger, and the firewood float is on the inside. From this dock, I can access the outer reaches of the firewood float and right up next to the cliff. I'm on a floating island that has a variety of protrusions that increase my surface area for fishing.

On the first cast from the end of the dock finger, I hook a 10-inch cutthroat, but I'm a long way from the pliers. The lure is a silver spinner with a single barbless hook, and the trout has swallowed the hook. Time is critical. I decide to take the fish to the Campion where a set of pliers awaits. The fish isn't keen on the trip and flops out of my hand onto the deck, the hook still attached in its mouth. I struggle with him on the wooden planks. He's making this tougher on himself than it should be.

Finally, in the Campion, I pry the hook loose with the pliers. There's no evidence of serious injury, so it's over the side for a quick release. But damage has been done (probably mostly shock from the extended time out of the water), and the trout rolls belly-up in the water – never a good sign. He floats out of reach, lying motionless on the surface. I am devastated, knowing I should have acted quicker and more efficiently. This fish could have been saved. He drifts out of reach.

The quickest rescue will be by the tin boat (more maneuverable and quickly untied), and I paddle rapidly to the site of the floating fish. I right the fish and push him forward in the water to get his gills working again. I gently press him underwater, and he wiggles and swims free, but he doesn't dart for the bottom. Instead, he swims smoothly (and obviously now recovered) only a few inches below the waterline, flying formation with the small boat. I've never seen this before – released trout usually dart for the bottom and away from the boat. I think he knows I care about him. He knows I have made an extra effort to save him. All his fins are moving smoothly – he looks like a tropical fish swimming slowly in an aquarium. He hovers just below the surface, swimming in parallel with the boat. Then he kicks with a healthy thrust and disappears into the depths of the Hole in the Wall.

\* \* \* \* \*

**I** have discovered that constant discussion about what lure to use is nearly meaningless to me. It seems that fish are determined to bite when they are ready, no matter what is offered to them. Then again, like most fishermen, I refuse to use anything except a few tradition-ally favorite lures. For me, that's a red-and-white daredevil (often orange-and-white in the local stores) or a silver spinning spoon (I prefer those with green feathers). This isn't meant to be expert ad-vice, since I tend to choose lures more for their weight than design or color; heavy lures are simply easier to cast.

For the real expert advice, I consult Julie, the waitress at the local coffee shop. She has demonstrated her prowess with large trout in Powell Lake repeatedly, including a recent prize-winning catch in a local fishing derby. Between delivery of plates of eggs and bacon, she offers straightforward advice that I take to heart. The rest of the morning clientele are listening intently, I'm certain, although they are not about to admit they can be outfished by a woman.

Powell Lake is better known for live bait, but I prefer artificial lures for simplicity. Trolling and mooching (jigging) seem to be more popular than casting, but I favor the exercise of casting and reeling in constantly, although trolling (or drift-casting) in my kayak is also enjoyable.

At the Shinglemill, you'll always find someone jigging off the docks. Early one morning, I am navigating down the lake, not pay-ing as much attention to my surroundings as I should. As I approach the marina at cruise power, I prepare to slow to a no-wake speed at the last minute. I don't see the fellow fishing on the corner dock of the marina until it is too late to avoid some wake in his spot. I reduce to full-idle quickly, and glance over my shoulder to see if the wake substantially disturbs his line. He starts reeling frantically as he catches a fish at this very moment. I watch him reel it in – a nice-sized... bullhead?

I have observed locals jigging off these docks for years, but I'm not sure what they are (or are not) catching. So after securing my boat, I walk over to the fisherman. I figure he won't be mad at me, since my boat's noise or wake may have stirred up his catch.

The fisherman's cute Cocker Spaniel comes out to greet me as I approach the end of the dock. I have observed both this fisherman and his dog at this same fishing spot on previous mornings. They seem to be a loyal team of man and dog that may be fishing as much for the atmosphere as the end product.

I inquire regarding the day's "luck," and the fisherman points to a plastic grocery bag (no need to stop fishing). I open the bag and find the 12-inch cutthroat trout I saw him catch (it's no bullhead) and a 15-inch rainbow. He explains that lots of feed permeates the water here: "Any of the docks are just as good.," he says. Today he is using a buzz-bomb, jigging at a depth of 30 feet. The bottom depth here is 60 feet.

"They go pretty deep in July," he explains. "I used to cast rather than jig, but my arm is a bit older these days."

He points to a wooden A-frame across the lower narrows that is one of his favorite fishing spots. He caught a 27-inch trout there a few days ago and regrets keeping it: "The big ones should be thrown back so they can spawn," he notes. He gave the big trout to a friend, and then returned to the same spot the next day to catch a 28-incher on his first cast. Partly atoning for his decision on the previous day, he released the large trout.

* * * * *

The good news is that it is pretty hard to lose lures in this lake, since the only major obstacles are the trees along the shoreline. The lake is so deep that it is nearly impossible to snag a lure on the bottom except near shore where underwater logs can intervene. A lost lure seems to occur only if it is the last lure in the boat or you just put on your favorite red-and-white. My preferred fishing spots are along steep cliffs, so the biggest problem is lure-eating-arbutus. How these beautiful red-bark trees grow out of dry rock is a marvel. Maybe they receive their nourishment from fishing lures.

One of my favorite activities is to paddle around the Hole in my kayak during calm conditions. Solo in the rear of this two-seater, I control my direction with the rudder (foot pedals), paddle a few strokes, and then drift a long way. With a fish pole sticking out, I am trolling as slow as is possible in any boat, and there's only the noise of the paddles to disturb the fish. I experience intermittent good luck with this method. The largest trout I catch in Powell Lake are via paddle-trolling in my kayak.

An even better method is to ride the Hole's flow, as it interacts with the water running through First Narrows. If I ride this flow, even paddling is not necessary (at least in one direction). With or without fishing "luck," it provides an enjoyable evening ride.

First Narrows is right around the corner and is an ideal fishing location. I find cutthroat trout on both sides of the narrows, but the far side near some granite cliffs provides me with the most fish.

There is, however, danger in crossing the Narrows. My kayak is large and bright yellow, and my life vest is vivid red. A tall-poled, Canadian flag flies from the stern. But powerboats traversing the narrows are not used to seeing kayaks here. I try to cross quickly, remembering what boaters in the nearby chuck dub kayaks: "speed bumps." There are two ways to interpret this terminology – kayaks cause powerboats to reduce speed; or powerboats just drive over them with a crunching "thump."

\* \* \* \* \*

All fishermen face a familiar problem: getting the fish off the hook. A three-hook lure can be particularly troublesome in this regard, and catch-and-release can be a disturbing experience when you know you have damaged a fish beyond the healing forces of nature. As a catch-and-release fisherman, I find this problem particularly troubling. John, as usual, comes to the rescue. He too is a catch-and-release guy, so he shows me how to crimp the barbs of new lures to eliminate (mostly) the barbs. It only takes a pair of pliers, and I'm immediately ready for barbless fishing. I lose more fish on barbless hooks, but catch-and-release fishermen are generally more tuned to the fight than the landing. This simple solution has made my fishing experiences in both fresh and salt water immensely more enjoyable.

The only significant problem that remains for me is bringing fish up from ocean depths. Too often they are severely injured during the decompression ride to the surface. One solution to this problem is to never fish in oceanic depths over 200 feet. That's hard to control in a dinghy or kayak without a depth finder. Too often, I reach the decompression limit without knowing it – and who says it's 200 feet? The amount of line needed to reach bottom is, of course, a good indicator, but it doesn't help much on the first cast. When fishing "luck" is good, that first throw might produce a deep-living fish.

Too often, I catch a beautiful red snapper (rockfish), only to find its swim bladder so bloated by the rise to the surface that it cannot submerge again after release. It takes all of the fun out of catch-and-release. One solution may be to immediately poke a small knife-hole in the protruding bladder when the fish surfaces. That may allow the fish to drop back into the shallow subsurface depths until the small wound heals and the fish can regain its deep habitat. Whether a deep-water fish is adaptable to shallow water on even a temporary basis is questionable, but I'm sure the small puncture in the bladder is not life threatening in itself. I've heard stories of red snapper being caught with evidence of a small healed puncture wound in their bladder, so that indicates that this technique may meet with at least limited success.

Maybe the only real solution is to revoke my personal catch-and-release rule for red snapper, but who is going to kill and clean them? On the other hand, when fishing the ocean, I find it essential to buy into the concept of nature's closed environment. There is a natural feeding cycle for all species. Even a dead, floating red snapper is not going to go to waste in this cycle. Eagles, seals, and other animals have to eat, and they will.

* * * * *

Twice while fishing (both times in the ocean) I experience a strange premonition regarding what I am about to haul aboard the boat. Such an instance occurs during my first visit to Theodosia Inlet. This trip is a solo overnight adventure in the Bayliner. After spending the night in Desolation Sound, I maneuver into Okeover and Lancelot Inlets the next morning. Okeover is not new to me (previously navigated by kayak), but I find Lancelot Inlet to be even more beautiful than expected. The waterway connection to Theodosia is a bit tricky for amateurs like me, and I am entering at low tide when the entry is most challenging.

I carefully slip into Theodosia, with my trusty boating guidebook, chart, and GPS under constant consultation. Halfway through the twisting passage, while I maneuver at a slow crawl, a logging workboat (a "crummy boat", as usual, far from crummy) is travelling in the opposite direction. It barrels around the corner as if this is a mile-wide river. The captain puts the boat into an impressive bank and waves to me, but I'm sure he is yelling "Damn Americans." When Canadians shout that popular refrain, it isn't critical to check the other boat's flag. It's just a good blanket assumption. However, in this instance, my flag is Canadian.

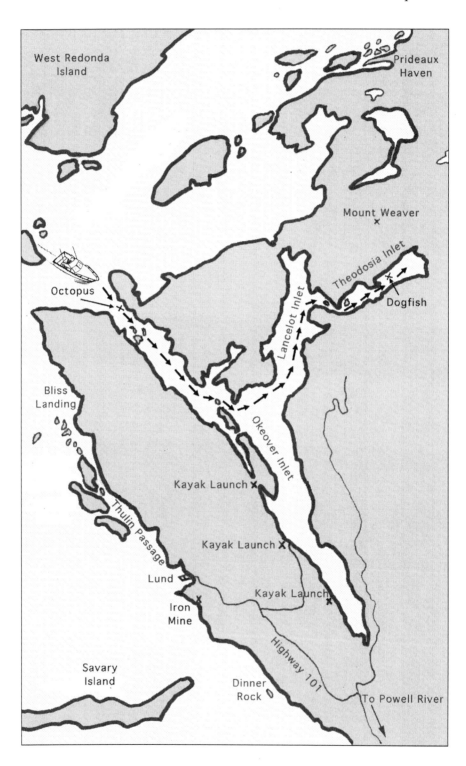

West Redonda
Island

Prideaux
Haven

Mount Weaver
×

Theodosia Inlet

Octopus

Dogfish

Lancelot Inlet

Bliss
Landing

Okeover Inlet

Kayak Launch ✗

Thulin Passage

Kayak Launch ✗

Lund

Kayak Launch ✗

Iron
Mine ×

Savary
Island

Highway 101

Dinner
Rock

To Powell River

Rounding the last twist in the entrance, Theodosia spreads out before me. This is my first visit to this historic logging inlet in any type of vehicle. I expect giant trees against the mountains. Instead, the area is now nearly denuded of trees. One of the biggest logging slashes in the region is just east of Theodosia. Another piece of this disappointment involves John's reports of the beauty of Theodosia, one of his favorite ATV destinations. It just doesn't live up to my expectations. It seems like a relatively boring, flat inlet. The following year I go into Theodosia with John, this time via quad. From the ground, the view is completely different than from the water. All is gorgeous, including the inlet (as seen from shore).

I've experienced similar letdowns when viewing the British Columbia coast from the air. It's beautiful, of course, but an airborne perspective includes a loss of appreciation regarding this area's size and scope. It is too easy to fly to Bute Inlet in my Piper Arrow (but impossible to land there). Flying is quick and efficient, but lacking in challenge. Try the same trip to Bute by boat – it consumes a full day, and you can't even conduct this trip via land.

The first time I fly over Okeover Inlet is a complete disappointment. The waters that I struggled with for hours in a kayak are transited in minutes in my Arrow. The surrounding mountains look puny, and I can easily see Powell Lake from my airborne perch over Okeover. The sense of remoteness and geographic viewpoint are completely lost rather than enhanced. Airplanes provide a great view, but that view is not necessarily the best perspective for appreciation of the bold landscape.

After entering Theodosia in the Bayliner, I buckle down for a demanding afternoon. After a simple anchoring exercise (my anchoring is usually not simple), I prop open the forward deck hatch, slip into the V-berth, and nap in the sun that is sneaking through the overhead opening.

Later, I prepare the dinghy (Mr. Bathtub) for a simple fishing exercise. I will motor to the center of the inlet where the water is respectfully deep for fishing, and see what I can catch.

You don't motor very fast in Mr. Bathtub, but when I find my selected fishing spot, it takes only a few casts to hook a good-sized fish. But it is a dogfish. The remarkable thing is that I know it is a dogfish the moment it hits my lure. Considering the variety of fish in these waters and my lack of fishing expertise, there is no way I can be sure this is a dogfish, but I am. I have caught only a few dog-fish previously, and I certainly am not able to identify it by the fight or any other aspect of hooking this fish. Maybe it is the fact that an immediate thought comes to my mind as the fish hits the lure. I play the scene forward: A fairly large fish comes aboard Mr. Bathtub; I reach for my needle-nose pliers to remove the hook, and… I imme-diately recognize that I have left my pliers back in the Bayliner.

What species of fish necessitates pliers to remove a hook more than a dogfish? Most dogfish are not large (typically a little over a foot long), but they have a scary shark mouth, to say nothing of their dorsal stinger. And getting a hook out without pliers will be tricky. Therein probably lies part of the reason I conclude it is a dogfish. It is the worst possible scenario.

The fish provides quite a fight, and when it surfaces, there is no surprise. It is a dogfish, and also of no surprise is the fact that it has swallowed the hook. I am not going into that mouth with my hand, so what to do? I decide to try towing the fish back to the Bayliner in Mr. Bathtub.

I lower the shark (about 18 inches long) back into the water and begin the long, slow journey to the Bayliner. The fish doesn't stop fighting for even a moment along the way. The struggling dogfish slows Mr. Bathtub even further – three horsepower versus the shark. After about 30 minutes, I step out of the dinghy onto the Bayliner's swim grid. Then, just when success is assured (the pliers are only a few feet beyond the swim grid), the dogfish disappears. Unfortu-nately, he bites through my 60-pound test line with those ugly teeth, rather than throwing off the hook. I don't mind losing the lure, but I feel terrible about sending the dogfish down to his ocean home with a lure in his mouth. After what that dogfish put me through, you'd think I'd feel less concerned, but it's never pleasant to think about a wounded animal, even an ugly one. I'm sure I could have retrieved that barbless hook with a pair of pliers.

The second fish I identify prior to seeing it surface is more unique. Guessing that a fish on the end of my line is a ling cod doesn't take a lot of imagination, since they are everywhere in these waters. But what about an octopus? (Okay, an octopus is not a fish, but you get the idea.)

This incident happens in Okeover Inlet on the very same trip. When you enter Okeover, the cliff walls on the north side beg to be fished. They simply look like fish heaven.

I pull up against the cliff and note another boat fishing the same area, less than a mile from my position. I drop my fishing line into 300 feet of water (no snapper, please) and start jigging. Almost immediately, I snag the bottom. I assume it is a sunken log rather than a rock because there seems to be a bit of give (not much). After trying the yank method until I have embedded the hook into the log even more, I begin to reposition the boat, hoping to back over the log (or rock) and pull the lure loose. And I do. But as I start to reel in my line (300 feet is a long way to reel), I realize that I am bringing part of the tree with me. The dead weight (not a fish) is bending my pole to its limit and stretching the line to the breaking point. But I keep reeling, hoping to recover my favorite lure. Then I notice some fish movement on my pole (not much), and it is at that point I know I have caught an octopus. And it is a big one.

Why I guess (know) it is an octopus is a mystery to me. But I simply know, and then I start planning how I am going to handle its arrival on the boat – or better yet, not handle it. This time my pliers stand ready, but what good will they be?

I hope the other boat (now drifting closer) sees the action in my boat – maybe he will come even closer to investigate. If he is watching my boat, he is certainly close enough to see the bent rod. Surely he (anyone) knows more about an octopus than I do, so he may be able to assist. As I begin taking satisfaction in the nearness of this boat in the otherwise remote landscape, the fisherman pulls in his line, cranks his engine, and departs.

Alone in Okeover with an octopus; better yet, an amateur American fisherman with relatively no ocean fishing experience alone in Okeover with an octopus. There must be some reason for me to "know" that I am reeling in an octopus, but the reasoning is certainly not evident. It is a dead weight that turns into live action on my line, although there are lots of fish that react this way – ling cod, to name one. And sea slugs are a creature that you can snag on the bottom;

they act as dead weight, but they remain inactive until they surface and you realize how ugly they are. I have never caught an octopus (never considered catching one), so there really is no precedent for my knowledge that this is the big day.

As I reel in my line, I consider the alternatives. I can cut the line, but how could I do that to any creature? Lugging a lure around in your mouth for the rest of your life is not a pleasant thought. I don't want to hurt this octopus, but I also don't want to deal with it.

Finally, after the long reeling process, the octopus appears off the side of the boat, still several feet below the surface. His tentacles swirl slowly in every direction, just like in the movies. He is huge (to me), five feet in diameter with his tentacles fully extended. And he is beautiful.

How can an octopus be so gorgeous? As he breaks the surface, the octopus retracts its tentacles toward his body, and they droop straight downward. His huge eyes stare directly at me, begging for mercy. His mouth is moving slowly, talking to me as best he can. He is clearly telling me not to be afraid, and that he is afraid of me. His color is the most gorgeous red that I have ever seen. Rust-red – no, almost brick-red. His skin is shining, and the suction cups on his tentacles pulse slowly. This is the most beautiful sea creature I have ever seen. And the hook is barely in his mouth. It looks like the octopus is holding onto the lure by suction alone.

I tell him to let go. He doesn't, so I tell him again, but I'm sure he holds on because he doesn't understand. His tentacles sway slowly every which way. I wonder if he can snap those legs toward me (it seems he can only control his tentacles in slow motion), and I speculate whether those pulsing suction cups can latch onto my body. But I do not fear him any longer.

I reach out with the pliers without fright. My pole bends sharply, the 60-pound-test line stretching to its limit. I grasp the hook with the pliers and twist gently. The octopus falls two feet to the water's surface with a giant splash. He remains there, right at the surface, for a few seconds, once again spreading his tentacles to their full extent. Reddish dye squirts out and begins spreading around him in a perfect circle. He is squirting "Hello," or "Thank you," or maybe

"See you again." Maybe he is squirting "Goodbye, friend." And then he unhurriedly sways his tentacles in a symphonic motion. The octopus gradually descends into the ocean, tentacles spread wide. I watch in awe as he slowly disappears into the sea.

# Chapter 9

## USO

When it becomes apparent that Powell River is going to be my home, I start reading as much about the history of the region as I can find. There are some good source materials available, but much of the older material is out-of-print. A visit to the town's library reveals a whole shelf of books that are appropriate for review. The Powell River Museum is another terrific source of historical documents. Their staff is willing to search for some out-of-print books that are not in the library. If anything turns up, they promise to notify me, and on several occasions they come through with some old books that hit the target.

One area that particularly interests me involves the mysteries of the region – old folklore and unsolved enigmas that surely would be documented in a region rich in historical character. I am especially interested in Powell Lake itself, and finally obtain a copy of *Mysterious Powell Lake* by Carla Mobley. The book, printed in 1984, is a collection of historical tales that I appreciate, but the stories aren't really mysteries of the type that most interest me. This book offers good information about local characters (not completely documented, as in any good mystery), but nothing about unexplained phenomena in the region. There simply must be legends regarding unexplained extraordinary events in an area such as this. Powell Lake itself, with its enormous depths, must have at least one sea monster.

When I come across reports of a sea monster in an old edition of the local newspaper (subsequently replaced by two newer local newspapers), I am thrilled. The monster, designated an Unidentified Swimming Object (USO), comes complete with old grainy photos that look like a dead whale that has decomposed for several weeks on a beach near Powell River. It is treated by the newspaper more as a joke than as a mystery – the sort of news that everybody takes lightly. Who would approach a decomposed whale for close inspection anyway?

Overall, the USO offers a moment of hope, followed by disappointment when the sightings are not mentioned in any modern material. Even if there is a USO, it sounds like the monster is long gone.

But Powell Lake is extremely deep, the remnant of an old fjord. I can't travel this lake by boat without reminding myself how far the lake floor extends below me. It's a feeling similar to flying in an airplane and (I don't recommend this) thinking about the thousands of feet of air between you and the ground. It's enough to curl the hair on the back of your neck.

There's a USO down there somewhere in Powell Lake, that's for certain.

\* \* \* \* \*

Indian lore permeates the region, and I'm proud to participate in some of the ceremonies that mark the local tribe, the Sliammon. Not unlike the relationship between loggers and all-terrain vehicle riders, there is a love-hate link between Caucasian locals and the Sliammon. Based on what I've seen elsewhere in Canada, including the arctic regions, the relationship here is one of the best possible.

Tribal lore is plentiful, and I never watch a raven (a bird of an-
cestral linkage for many Canadian native cultures) without wondering whose Indian soul is in the sky today. John doesn't necessarily
feel the same way, probably tainted by a few run-ins with ravens.
One day, when visiting me at Number 3, John returns to his boat
to find that our local raven has chomped through part of his boat's
canvas top, trying to get at his lunch. On another occasion, our raven (who never bothers me) attacks John's backpack at Number 2,
directly across the bay from my cabin. The raven loses major points
with this assault, since Bro's lunch is in the backpack. Mess with
John, if you must, but never mess with Bro.

＊ ＊ ＊ ＊ ＊

One April, I arrive at the Hole in the Wall to hear, on the first
evening of a week-long visit, a strange thumping noise in the distance. It is difficult to identify where the sound originates, although
it seems concentrated in the back bay of Number 2 cabin across
the Hole. The sound shifts with the wind, sometimes sounding as
far away as the headlands overlooking First Narrows. It's a noise
that is both eerie and annoying. I would best equate it to the sound
of a boat  protective fender being whacked by the waves – an artificial, plastic sound. On the other hand, it also echoes like native war
drums. I prefer to hear it as native drums rather than as a discarded
plastic fender.

   That night, on the float during my middle-of-the-night star
check, the Hole is completely silent. But the sound returns the
following evening, and its location is again difficult to pinpoint.
I launch my kayak under the pretext of fishing in the last light
of twilight. In reality, I am trying to pinpoint the source of the
thumping. First, I paddle through John's back bay, finding
nothing unusual in the water. As I drift-cast out of Hole in the
Wall toward the Narrows, the thumping is definitely to the south,
seeming to move from Number 2's bay (at the start of my kayak
jaunt) to the sandy beach near First Narrows. By the time I reenter
the Hole, the sound is gone. I give it a name: "Thumper."

   For the remainder of my week's stay, Thumper comes and goes.
Not surprising, it seems related to the wind. A little wind from any

direction sets Thumper in motion, and that indicates (to me) something riding the waves at the shoreline, bouncing and thumping. My binoculars scan every nook and cranny of the Hole, looking for anything out of place. I expect to find a boat fender whacking against a log. That's the perfect explanation for this sound. But I have not discarded thoughts of native war drums and ghosts from the region's history.

Thumper is still going strong when I push off my float to catch the airline flight home.

* * * * *

Two months later, I step onto my float on a Friday evening, and the first thing I hear is Thumper. Flotsam moves around this lake continually, and seldom does it stay put for long. But Thumper is still making noise, no louder, but now more sinister by nature of its persistence. The next morning, in character with my previous bout with Thumper, there is no noise, but the thumping returns that evening as a light wind picks up.

Calm conditions and moderate or greater winds send Thumper into hibernation. In light winds, the noisy spirit thrives. A change in wind direction does not eliminate Thumper, but such changes seem to alter its location. The noise is so faint (or distant) that I have to strain to hear it. If it weren't so silent in the Hole, I'd never hear it in the first place. This continues for several more weeks.

One day, John arrives at Number 2 by an unusual route. He and three other quad riders (plus one motorcyclist) pop out of (seemingly) nowhere onto his cabin's front porch in the early afternoon. When occupants arrive at a float cabin, there is plenty of warning, since the prerequisite boat must arrive first. But on this day, John and his friends simply hop down onto the porch from the land bridge.

There is a new logging road that now connects Theodosia Inlet to Powell Lake's Chippewa Bay. From Chippewa, it is a short quad ride to the nearly-overgrown logging road behind Number 2. John has celebrated this new route by clearing a trail from the deteriorated road to his cabin. It isn't exactly national park quality, but the trail to his cabin is navigable, if you know how to find it. I mourn the connection of Hole in the Wall to the outside world, but

Theodosia isn't exactly a tourist destination, so the rough logging road probably won't sport anything other than logging trucks and quads for many decades.

As strange as it is to see people pop up out of nowhere onto John's float (preceded, of course, by the roar of quad engines), I am ready for them. John told me about the indoctrination of this new quad route, and I have a plan to greet the riders. I hop aboard my kayak with a large bag of popcorn, prepared earlier in the morning, and paddle to Number 2, serving as the welcoming party for the riders. Everyone except John and Bro receive my arrival at Number 2 less than enthusiastically, probably because the riders are exhausted after the long trip from Theodosia. There is no danger of tourists arriving via road this year. The popcorn goes nearly untouched, but everyone seems to appreciate my effort.

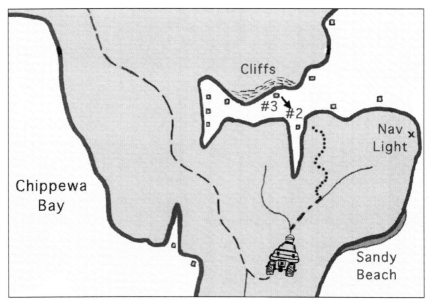

After their lunch-stop at the cabin, I follow the group as they climb the cliff trail to their bikes. Bro needs an ass-push up the steep wooden steps. The end-of-trail area above Number 2 is narrow, so it takes some time to get the vehicles turned around. John has his machete standing ready to preen his new trail some more on the way out.

The riders depart in a roar of engines, climbing the rough trail back to the logging road, with John's machete whacking the branches, and Bro in his quad aft-passenger box hanging on for dear life.

John's horn blasts a good-bye, and I wave from the grove of trees that marks the end of the improvised parking area. There is no way John can see my wave, but it doesn't matter. For a few minutes, I stand in the small grove of trees, replanted after logging activity many years ago. I listen to the engines rounding the bend and dropping into the lowlands at the back-end of the Hole. The motors echo off the mountain wall of Chippewa Bay, and John honks to me one more time. I listen until I hear the engines no more. And then I hear Thumper.

He is directly overhead. I look up, and tree branches merge in a mass of green – tall, lean trees so close to each other that their small trunks are nearly rubbing each other. In fact, some of these tall, thin pecker poles are whacking gently together at the top – thump, thump, thump. Now they stop waving in the breeze, and the sound moves to the next grove just beyond the ridge to the south. Thump, thump.

Now when I hear Thumper from my float, it is no longer a mystery. Instead of an annoying "thump," I hear a beautiful natural sound. It is a sound that I will never find tiring. And I was right all along – it is the sound of native spirits in the trees.

\* \* \* \* \*

Fog is not common on Powell Lake. Low stratus clouds are plentiful, but they seldom stretch to the ground. I've seen fog on the lake only a few times, and I remember my first encounter as a mysterious phenomenon. Since I'm a pilot who has lived with fog for decades (Los Angeles is famous for advection fog), it's unusual for me to designate a foggy day as particularly mysterious. But it felt that way.

The mysterious feeling was undoubtedly compounded by my first encounter with fog in a boat. I've taken off in aircraft during nearly zero visibility quite a few times, and flying in stratus clouds for hours – not an uncommon experience – is technically the same as flying in fog. Fog is a stratus cloud that extends to the ground.

On this particular evening, Margy and I really want to get to the cabin. It is one of those short visits to Powell River, and we relish every moment on our float. But when we arrive at the Shinglemill, the visibility is much lower than we've ever experienced previously. I can barely see across the lower narrows from the marina. But we can proceed slowly and turn back if the conditions worsen; sucker holes are rationalized away, as they often are. We decide to cling to the west shoreline (the marina side of the lake), since it looks like we will lose sight of the shore by crossing to the east. That was our second mistake; the first was departing in the first place.

My familiarity with the west shoreline is minimal. The other shore is the standard route, since the waves there are typically less intense, and I always want to check out John's lower-lake cabins, Number 4 and Number 1, along the way. (He'll never change that numbering system until I'm finally used to it.) When John is on the lake, that's the route he takes too, so we sometimes conduct mid-lake meetings along the way – two boats rafted together, discussing our latest projects.

As we reach One-Mile Bay, the fog worsens to the point that I decide to dip into the bay to keep the shoreline in sight. Oops – a log breakwater and orange cones come into view rather unexpectedly in the fog. The bay is the water supply for the Wildwood community above the cliffs, and this is a keep-out warning. We slip along parallel to the breakwater, a good navigational landmark.

After that, conditions go rapidly downhill. We travel at a snail's pace, eventually at idle RPM in forward gear, barely moving. The shore is primarily cliffs without waterline obstacles. But every once in awhile, only a few feet offshore, a log snag appears, reminding me how little I know about this edge of the lake. I move outward another 10 feet and lose contact with the shore. It is then that I think about other boaters who might elect to return from their cabins via this same shoreline. I honk my horn every few minutes to warn other boats, and the echoes from the cliffs add to the eerie feeling that is building within me.

Margy is always helpful in instances such as this, since she lends me confidence in the worst possible predicaments. We've been together in a variety of adrenaline-producing situations in small airplanes, and she is at her strongest when the situation is the worst (afterwards, she's a wreck). Margy is in the bow, calling out any obstacles she sees well before they become a problem.

I vary our course considerably to follow every indentation in the shoreline. What seems like a relatively straight shore is actually a long meandering noodle. Already we have spent longer than the typical 20-minute ride to the cabin, and we haven't even reached Three-Mile Bay. The bay is only about a mile and a half up the lake from the Shinglemill. In fact, it is not three miles from anything. How it got its name is beyond me. John says it might be three miles from the dam, but no one seems to care why it is so named. For me, everything centers around the Shinglemill, so that is my reference for most distances on the lake. Some locals use nearby Mowat Bay as their launching point, so they consider their world similarly focused there. The dam and paper mill are south of the Shinglemill and the bridge, so you tend to forget they exist. (The occupants of the old boathouses in that area would take exception to such an analysis.)

Three-Mile Bay is going to be a problem, since keeping the shoreline in sight will require deviating deep into this large indentation, and impatience is starting to become an issue. Try traveling at two knots in a boat for awhile, and see how long you last. It reminds me of trolling at its worst.

An added problem, the lack of sunlight, is becoming critical. Of course, there is little light in the fog, but night fog would be way beyond my limits. Sunset is only a half hour away, a factor that I had not considered when departing the Shinglemill. That was the third mistake.

The first float cabin off the point at Three-Mile Bay appears to our left (we are right off his front porch), and I decide to cut across the bay in the interest of time. I take a heading that seems appropriate, and within a few seconds all landmarks disappear into the fog. I'm sure that my horn blasts every few seconds are appreciated by residents in the nearby cabins.

It works out nearly perfect. We hit landfall just inside the promontory on the other side and adjust our course to follow the shore northward. We aren't yet even close to the mid-point of the route

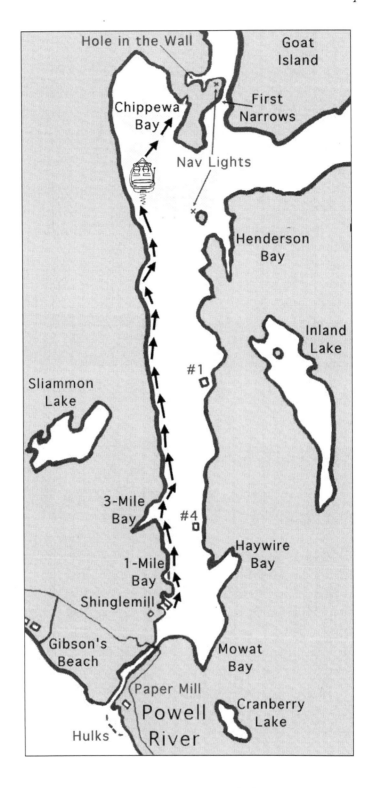

to our cabin, and my watch indicates it's approximately sunset. We decide to press on rather than turn back – the fourth mistake.

It is excruciatingly slow, as the fog gets even thicker, further intensified by the evening plunge through the dewpoint. There are times when I can't distinguish the trees at all. I edge a little closer to the shore, and suddenly see giant trees where I know smaller trees prevail. The trees are close and thus out of proportion. I try to maintain a distance from shore that allows me to barely see the outline of the vegetation (a gray-green blur) so that deeper water is guaranteed. What isn't guaranteed is the actual depth under the waterline at this close distance to shore.

We continue northward, eventually reaching headlands that I estimate as the edge of Chippewa Bay. There is really no way to know for sure where we are. But time, speed, and distance, coupled with my limited knowledge of this shore of the lake, make it seem logical that this is the promontory at the edge of Chippewa.

Margy and I discuss our perceptions briefly, agreeing that it seems like we were entering Chippewa Bay, and I make the turn to the northeast. Here is a tricky decision that has its pluses and minuses. There is no way we are going all the way around this huge bay with darkness approaching, but I don't want to turn too far to the right and completely miss the other side of the bay. It is open water to the east of Chippewa, and that means getting very lost. So I pick a compromise heading that seems to guarantee landfall well inside the far tip of the bay.

As we start across Chippewa Bay (or what we think is the bay), I begin to consider logging boats. This is the time of day they start home, and Chippewa Bay contains a major logging dock. These are the fastest boats on the lake, and they are in a hurry to get to dinner. Even in marginal weather conditions, they point their bow and go, using radar to keep them clear of the cliffs in low visibility and at night. Radar probably works a lot better at seeing cliffs than small boats. And would they even suspect that American city-folk are in the middle of Chippewa Bay on a day (night) like this? For the next 20 minutes, I listen intently for engines, but I'm not sure I will hear them over the idle of the Campion until it is too late. And if I do hear them, then what? The best way to keep my confidence from totally crumbling is to blast my horn every few seconds. But

I doubt these workboats would hear a puny horn over the roar of their diesels at full-throttle.

In the middle of the bay (by my rough time estimate), it is very lonely. I'm glad Margy is with me, because I feel totally detached from the earth. Maybe there is a reason those cartoon photos of heaven  show angels engulfed in clouds. Even the inside of a cloud as viewed from an airplane is not nearly as disorienting as this. Airplanes have instruments to trust. Here is nothing to refer to except a compass (with a nearly randomly selected heading) and a clock that is running discouragingly slow. Our boat is nearly stopped, and time is almost at a standstill. I am currently experiencing a phenomenon – whether it is best considered a natural or man-made phenomenon is tough to call, but a phenomenon it is. I am stranded in space and time.

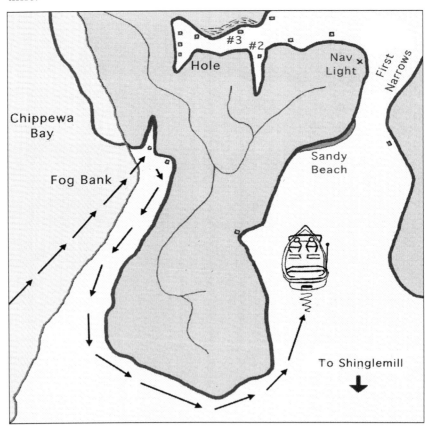

After an appropriate amount of time (now seeming in suspension), I begin to worry about my selection of heading. There is no shore in sight, and we have been plowing forward for what seems like an eternity. Have we missed the edge of the bay, and are we now driving hopelessly out into the open waters south of Goat Island? As much as I want to reach shore quickly, I slow the boat even further by coming out of gear every few seconds. That's the only way to reduce to dead slow with these dual props. My newest fear is that the fog is so thick (no way to tell how thick it is when you're in the middle of it) that we will smack into the cliffs on the other side of the bay with absolutely no warning.

My latest theory is that our horn will echo off the cliffs and may provide a few seconds warning of the collision, so now the horn is blaring even more frequently. There's nothing like loud, obnoxious noise when you already have a dozen reasons to sustain a tension headache.

Nearly simultaneously, two things happen. Float cabins appear directly off our bow. There are only a few cabins in Chippewa Bay (the waves are often a major problem here), and all cabins are in the same area. I know exactly where I am.

The second thing that happens at nearly the same instant is a mystery. The shoreline beyond the cabins is perfectly clear. Although daylight is rapidly fading, there is plenty of light against the forest, when compared to the nonexistent visibility within the fog. The term fog "bank" applies here. We are at the end of that bank, and beyond it is perfectly clear sky.

It is true that fog has to end somewhere, and often it is a very distinct end. But I've seen fog many times before, and there never was fog so joyously ended as this. There is really no mystery at all. It is just good ol' Mother Nature, playing her little tricks. But for me, I enjoy the resolution of enigmas.

There are no boats at the float cabins off our bow (no one is home), and the fog problem has been immediately resolved, so I blast three honks of the horn into clear air. I want Mother Nature to know we are now safely on the last leg of our journey home.

✳ ✳ ✳ ✳ ✳

One day while swimming in the natural pool behind our cabin, Margy decides to swim around the entire float. It's not a lengthy swim, but neither of us has done it before. Why leave the protection of our beautiful natural swimming pool? She circles counter-clockwise (Canadian anti-clockwise) past the kayak dock and then around our boat parked on the breakwater-side of the cabin. As she passes behind the boat, I hear a "Yipe!" To this day, Margy maintains that something grabbed her foot with a gentle tug as she swam behind our boat, and she's convinced it was the USO. But it was obviously just saying "Hello," because there was only a quick grab and then a release. It is solid proof that there is a USO in Powell Lake and it is, not surprisingly, a friendly leg-pulling monster.

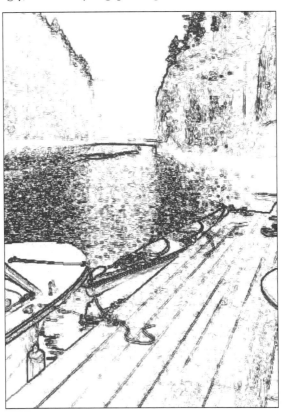

◊ ◊ ◊ ◊ ◊ ◊

# Chapter 10

# Quad Acrophobia

I accomplished one of the things that flight instructors are generally advised not to pursue: I taught my wife how to fly. The common recommendation within the industry is to turn that job over to another flight instructor. It is not unlike the concept of teaching your spouse to drive. Let someone else accept responsibility for the eruptions that can occur on both sides when such a task is undertaken with a spouse.

But it worked. There were no major confrontations, and we both learned a lot in the process. On one of her first solo cross-country flights, 10 hours of which are required for a private pilot certificate in the U.S., I listened on a portable VHF radio as she returned from Santa Barbara. I've always taught student pilots to confess their status on their first call to air traffic control on cross-country flights. It seems to slow the pace (and increase the patience) of radio calls the moment the controller knows a new pilot is involved.

"Brackett Tower, Cessna 714 Golf Mike, student pilot, over Eastland Shopping Center with Information Foxtrot." Margy's initial call is flawless. Right on! I'm cheering her on from my living room.

"Cessna Four Golf Mike, good afternoon. I'm a student controller," is the rather unorthodox reply. "Plan left traffic, Runway Two-Six Left. Report downwind." The controller sounds pleased he has found a fellow aviation student.

"Four Golf Mike will report downwind for Runway Two-Six Left," states Margy.

I laugh. This should be interesting. Student pilot and student controller. God help us all.

"Four Golf Mike, would you like a tour of the tower after landing?" inquires the controller. I'm not sure whether he is genuinely interested in this student's progress or simply hitting her up for a date.

"Negative. I can't. But thanks anyway," replies Margy.

I know Margy, and I know exactly what she means. But the controller doesn't get the picture.

"Oh, sure you can," he says in a cheerful voice. "Just use the telephone at the base of the control tower, and I'll buzz you in."

"No, I mean I can't come up those control tower stairs," replies Margy. She sounds more irritated now. I can imagine her, as a student pilot, trying to run her landing checklist, while this guy is forcing a conversation as she enters the downwind leg. She's not about to explain her declined invitation over the radio in more detail. It's bad enough to admit her fear of climbing the control tower steps to herself. To broadcast it to the world is not her idea of fun. Talk about student pilot pressure.

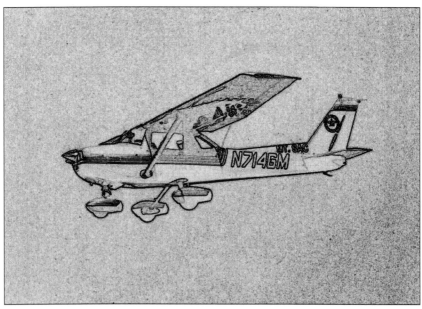

\* \* \* \* \*

John understands about as much as the student controller, although Margy tries to explain it to him.

"How can someone who flies airplanes be afraid of heights?" he asks while trying to coax Margy around the bend on Rainbow Main.

"I don't know. It's just not the same," says Margy, too frightened to muster a reasonable answer. She maneuvers the quad excruciatingly slow around the corner, top speed one-half klick, with an intensity of concentration that surpasses a racecar driver at 200 miles per hour. She has angled her quad to the extreme right side of the road, as far from the drop-off as possible.

We've been through this before, and John is convinced that his abrupt throw-it-at-her method will work on a quad. Rainbow Main sports a direct drop-off to Powell Lake. Beautiful to most; a complete horror show to Margy.

When lesser challenges arise (walking down a boat ramp at Westview Harbour during low tide), John can't understand it, as Margy comes to an abrupt and frightened halt. He isn't exactly the most understanding guy in the world. In instances like this, John's advice is often captured by his singular phrase: "Get over it."

Margy isn't going to get over it, and it has become a problem in her quad riding. You go places on a quad to witness the beauty of the steeply sloped landscapes. John is drawn to the steepest.

Margy loves to ride, but she hates the agony that sets in when her heart rises into her throat and she can hardly breathe. She also stops talking at moments like these, and John has little patience for such situations. In a nutshell, Margy comes to a screeching halt both physically and mentally when confronted with steep drop-offs, and John just pushes her harder when she is most afraid. You might call it a student-teacher standoff.

It's a unique fear of heights, since Margy flies airplanes. I can understand it because I too am a bit afraid of heights. But there is a difference in airplanes. It's not the same as standing on top of a tall building and looking over the side and seeing the structure that supports you, or looking down off a high bridge (which I too avoid). There are variations to the phobia that is generally classified as fear of heights. If you have claustrophobia, don't set foot in an airplane. If you have a fear of heights, acrophobia, you may become a pilot. When it comes to heights, I prefer to refer to Margy's anomoly as "altophobia," and it only pertains to being on terra firma.

Margy is determined. This fear has followed her for years. I believe she actually closes her eyes when she drives over high freeway overpasses in Los Angeles, which is why I prefer to drive when I am with her. At least I don't close my eyes on freeways. But now she has an important reason to conquer this fear – she wants to ride her quad, and John goes to high places.

\* \* \* \* \*

"**W**ith you in this condition, where can we go?" asks John disgustedly. It's a rhetorical question, muttered without patience for the patient.

"Just keep it kind of flat," replies Margy.

"Kinda flat?!" retorts John. "Everywhere around here has some height. Do you want to drive back and forth along Duck Lake?"

"That would be fine, as a matter of fact," notes Margy.

Actually, she would enjoy that. She definitely doesn't need vertical challenges to gain satisfaction. Yet, she is quite good at handling her quad during a climb, as long as there is no drop-off to the side that she can see. At Giovanni Lake (not "Giovanno!"), she climbs in and out without a problem. The climb is rugged and steep at times, but there are no cliffs to the side. Give her a visible drop-off, and she immediately goes into her slow motion act, creeping along at a snail's pace. It's agonizing to watch, especially when John is providing his standard helpful advice: "Get over it."

"How do you fly airplanes?" asks John again.

"That's different," replies Margy.

"Different?" snips John. "How is it different?"

"It really is different," I note. "She's got a unique case of quad altophobia. She's the same way on bridges and steep stairs."

"Oh," replies John. He obviously doesn't get it.

Margy formulates a plan to "get over it." But it is not the same as John's immersion method. At home in Los Angeles, she schedules an appointment with one psychiatrist, then another. She goes through "psychos" like water. One wants to talk endlessly about her childhood. Another has never faced a client with this kind of problem and seems oblivious to handling the situation. And then there is Mr. Fix-It Man.

Mr. Fix-It Man starts out, like the rest, wanting to talk about her childhood, but pretty soon he is reading up on similar cases and getting innovative. By week number three, they are riding escalators at the local mall. Or at least one of them is riding escalators, while Margy stares down and sneaks away from the edge. But Mr. Fix-It Man is persistent. His office moves to the mall, and they meet before each lesson at the food court, where he gets his favorite snack. Eating burgers and riding up and down escalators for $90 an hour is a pretty good deal. It's a good deal for Margy too – she's actually getting fixed.

Slowly, over a period of weeks, she's actually getting onto escalators. Every chance she gets, she does her assigned homework, often dragging me along to ride up and down. We try new escalators too. Some of them she conquers, others she doesn't. But I see definite improvement. She's not ready for Rainbow Main or Tin Hat, but there is noticeable progress.

Mr. Fix-It Man has a variety of special methods, including diversionary tactics of discussing strange mechanical emergencies in aircraft. As it turns out, he is a pilot too, constantly worrying about what to do if the prop departs the airplane. Since Margy has more flying experience than he does, he uses the $90 sessions to discuss the asymmetrical forces that would tear the engine off its mounts if the prop cracks and throws a blade. He wants to know if it can be tested in a simulator. Maybe Mr. Fix-It Man needs a fix-it man.

Knowing nothing about matters of the mind, both Margy and I think hypnosis has promise. Mr. Fix-It Man discusses hypnosis, seems to utilize it in other situations, but never uses it on Margy. You can't tell the psycho how to psycholize, so she doesn't try. But we know that John's dad, Ed, is an amateur hypnotist. I can just imagine asking Ed to hypnotize Margy. When he's finished, she'll sit up, bark, and sing the Canadian national anthem.

One of Margy's sessions involves Mr. Fix-It Man riding right seat in her Ford Mustang as she attempts to climb the winding road to Mount Baldy. He's a braver man than I am.

Inch-by-inch, Margy's escalator rides become easier, or at least she makes the rides look easier. It's time for some careful tests on her quad.

* * * * *

In July, we go on our first quad ride since the Los Angeles "treatment" designed to cure Margy of her fear of heights. We don't expect miracles, but it would be nice to see noticeable progress on the quad rather than only on escalators. The real test will be whether John notices a change. He's pretty skeptical.

We depart for the Bunster Range, a line of mountains separating Sliammon Lake from Theodosia Valley and Chippewa Bay. This is a route that John and his brothers have been working on lately in an attempt to blaze a quad trail that will allow nearly direct access to Hole in the Wall. So far, they have turned back several times in their attempts to connect to the logging road on the south side of Chippewa.

The going is rugged in an area of swampy ponds and thick forest. But John thinks they only need to conquer a 2-mile stretch to join the logging road on the other side. On each end of this unexplored segment is a tame logging road.

There is a big difference between hiking on established trails and hiking through dense growth. John's brother, Dave, says that their previous failures to get through this section mean that today is pretty much the last chance. John immediately christens the still-to-exist new route "Last Chance Trail."

As usual, our first stop is at the gas station. At one point, we have two pumps running simultaneously, pumping gas into John's truck and three quads in-order. In the adjacent pump aisle, John gets the chance to discuss the latest news with a friend gassing up his boat and then with Eric who pulls in to fill up his truck.

Eric is intimately familiar with the Bunster Range. In fact, he is the original driving force behind finding a route through the Bunsters, and he is thrilled that John has not given up on the project. This chance meeting at a gas station is an unexpected coincidence, a reminder of how small this town really is, and a routine example of how many of the local residents know John.

Eric leaves before we are finished filling our quads, smiling about what will happen if John and his brothers are successful today. The next step will be almost immediate – the Powell River ATV Club will be quick to grasp the opportunity to build a trail connecting the two logging roads. If they don't act quickly, John and his brothers will do the work themselves. This will be no minor construction job, but it will be a straightforward task after the trail is blazed.

Bro is not with us today. He's recovering from the ride on the previous day. Bro is not pleased regarding missing today's quad ride, and John already feels guilty for leaving him behind. But I am putting two-plus-two together into a pleasant conclusion: We will be home early today.

Before leaving the gas station, John rechecks the tiedowns on our quads. He is not happy with the arrangement, since we came up short on the number of straps needed for three quads (my quad and Margy's on the trailer and John's in the bed of his pickup). The two quads on the trailer are tied together to make up for the shortage of straps, a barely acceptable arrangement.

We exit Highway 101 north of Powell River on Wilde Road, climbing to our off-load spot adjacent to Sliammon Lake, near a yellow triangular sign proclaiming: "Wilderness Forest Service Road – Not Maintained." Rick is already parked and ready to ride, although he left home after us. He always wins the race.

As we prepare to off-load our quads, Dave arrives in his truck. It's clear that our three-quad trailer train will slow the flow of things, so I quickly remove the tiedown straps, install the metal ramps, and hop aboard my Kodiak to start the off-load process. When I start the engine and shift into reverse, my quad barely moves. I give it a little more gas, but I catch my error before pulling Margy's quad with me. The connection tiedown strap needs to come off first. "Go slow" is always a good procedure at times like this. We've not even started our ride, and I've screwed up already. But it is my lucky day – John is busy with his quad and fails to notice my error. I can't believe I actually get away with something for a change.

I am the last out of the parking area, since I insist on powering up my GPS to check the parking spot's location. Today will be my first supervised solo. John, Dave, and Rick will attempt to blaze the new trail, but I won't be joining them. Margy is nursing a sprained ankle, so this is no day for hiking, especially on an off-trail trudge. So Margy and I will ride to the trailhead with the brothers and then go our separate ways.

Thus, my concern with our GPS starting point. Getting lost would be far worse than a forgotten tiedown strap. I get a firm fix on the parking spot, presented clearly on the GPS as an easy-to-identify curve on the road.

I am finally under way, catching up to John, Dave, Rick, and Margy at a turnoff a few klicks up the road where they wait for me.

During the climb into the Bunsters, we make several stops for John to point out landmarks to guide Margy and me on our by-ourselves excursion. I pay particular attention to my surroundings, since I have become complacent by always following John and depending on his flawless navigation.

I ride in fourth position, Dave following behind me. There is little dust today, so we ride close enough that I can see John and Rick at the front of our five-ship formation, weaving their bikes in an intricate pattern of lateral crisscross choreography on the narrow road. There are no riders more experienced in this area, and today John is enjoying the added maneuverability he can exercise without Bro in his traditional aft box. The two brothers interlace their paths back-and-forth smoothly like a military flight formation team. I know the way they drive, and I know they are now maintaining a continuous conversation as they ride in this intricate pattern, similar to friends conducting a routine evening chat on the telephone.

The climb continues upward at a fairly constant rate, easy riding slowed occasionally by mud-soaked trenches. We break out into an extensive logging slash, the type that often marks the end of the road. Not surprising, the forest stops us at a series of dirt hillocks at the far northern tip of the slash. It's the end of the road. And the beginning of the prospective Last Chance Trail.

As John and his brothers gather their gear for the trek into the woods, I turn on my GPS receiver and wait for the satellites to respond. I show the display to Dave, and he calls Rick and John over to see the moving map. They never refer to a GPS when riding or hiking, since they need no such aids. But the GPS displays the end of the road clearly. It shows the road they are trying to connect with, and it displays the challenging valley they will be entering. There are several small ponds and a creek in a pattern that Rick recognizes from their previous unsuccessful attempts to get through. The GPS map assists them little in their plans today, but they spend a few minutes commenting on how it confirms what they already know. The bottom line is they are about to enter a dense spot in the forest, with obstacles that include severely swampy terrain and slopes that will be difficult to access by quad. They know exactly what they are getting into, and it isn't going to be easy.

John provides me with a few last-minute suggestions regarding places Margy and I can safely explore, and he reminds us to be careful. That is one reminder that is not necessary. My first supervised solo includes a hearty respect for the power of the environment.

We watch the brothers disappear on foot into the forest, carrying clippers, chainsaw, and an abundance of hot pink trail marking tape. Mosquitoes buzz around our heads, focused on the only two people remaining. It's time to get moving.

The day is full of wonder for two novice quad riders finally on their own. John has taught us well. We know our limitations, and that is the most important lesson of all. We confidently motor across the connection road to Okeover Inlet, stopping at a scenic spot overlooking the narrow stretch of ocean. Margy parks close to the downslope at the side of the road. This is the new Margy, and we both know it. I take her picture here, the first time I have ever seen her looking comfortable near a drop-off. She'll need to send this photo to Mr. Fix-It Man.

After a lunch stop at Okeover Inlet, I fish in a prospective creek (no fish, but that doesn't matter). While I am below the bridge in a promising-looking spot, I gaze back up to see… Now this may not seem remarkable, but Margy is sitting on the wooden bridge railing, feet hanging below, looking down at me. This is not something to expect from an acrophobic. In fact, it is a benchmark of her progress and no small accomplishment.

We climb up the road John has identified as leading to Chippewa Lake, a challenging gradient with deeply rutted cross-trenches. We break out into a large logging slash that includes a steep drop-off to the picturesque lake. Margy doesn't come to her customary crawl, but simply motors on without hesitation. She is cured! (Well, let's say the improvement is significant.)

We pause at the side of the road for a quad altophobia victory photo. Margy poses with her arms outspread in a gesture of celebration. Mr. Fix-It Man would be proud.

Returning downhill from Chippewa Lake, I follow Margy as we cross the granite outcrops that quickly lead to the muddy cross-trenches. For awhile, I follow only a few feet behind her, but displaced to the left side of the road. Suddenly, I notice that all of Margy's front and rear wheels are locked as she continues down a not-so-steep grade. Yet her tires do not seem to be sliding across the ground. Instead they appear to be gliding a fraction of an inch above the surface. This isn't an out-of-control skid, and it isn't a very steep slope, but she has locked the wheels, and she is not stopping. Her quad is simply sliding smoothly ahead. What is going on?

Like a huge chicken laying a mighty big egg, a multi-faced boulder pops out from below the rear of her quad. It is at least a foot in diameter and almost cube-shaped. Her bulletproof oil pan has been riding on this flat rock for the past few feet, sliding her quad gently down hill. Locking the brakes does nothing except make Margy feel like she is in charge. The boulder, rather than her steering and brakes, determine her directional fate, but now she is free to ride again. ("I knew what was happening when I heard my quad bottom out," she says later. "But I worried only about how I was going to explain this equipment abuse to John.")

After a stop at Sliammon Lake to try a few casts with my collapsible fishing rod (once again, no luck – no worries), we arrive uneventfully at our original off-load spot. It's only a short wait until Rick arrives (first, as always) to tell us about the fate of the new trail.

Success! There were some challenges, but they made it through the new Last Chance Trail and celebrated with lunch on the logging road on the other side. There are some very muddy spots that will require log foundations, and a creek will have to be forded or a bridge constructed. One area will require a switchback, but the route will work.

The day of accomplishment ends with a leisurely drive home. John is pleased with the prospects of the new trail, but he is even prouder when he hears my accounts of Margy sitting on the edge of the bridge and not slowing down at the drop-offs.

"I knew you could do it," he says proudly. "Like I said, you just needed to push a little harder... and get over it."

John above Alpha Lake in late June, with snow to left. Trail to right winds in along Stillwater Main and E-Branch. This photo was taken on the hiking trail to Beta Lake.

Bro in his quad box, wearing his raincoat and ready to ride. The box is mounted on the aft end of a 660cc Grizzly. Fully carpet walls and floor, of course.

Margy in front seat of 22-foot Libra XT kayak at the Iron Mine, near Lund. A fishing pole fits in the cylinder at lower left for trolling from the right side of the kayak. Photo taken en route to Savary Island.

The Maithus brothers at Murphy Lake. Left to right: John, Dave, Rick, and Rob. The quad is a Kodiak. Yes, John is holding a piece of chicken, which he refused to relinquish for the photo.

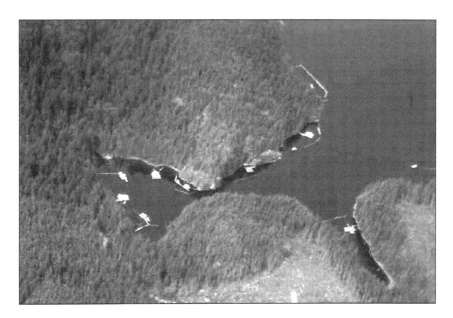

Hole in the Wall, looking north. Cabin Number 2 is in the bay at lower right, with Number 3 across from it. Photo taken from Piper Arrow in 2003. Top right cabin in far inland end of the Hole has since been removed.

Westview, with marina, airport (center of photo) and West (Hammil) Lake to right. Powell Lake is out of sight to left. North Harbour (left) houses private boats. Ferries and commercial boats dock in South Harbour.

*112*

Author with cutthroat trout, approximately 100 feet from Cabin Number
3. Vertical granite cliffs like these are favorite fishing spots on Powell Lake.
Photo courtesy of David Franklin, who catches miniature trout.

John and Bro in tin boat, southbound on Powell Lake near Clover Lake,
following a hike with the author to the small lake on Goat Island.

# Chapter 11

## Endless Summer

It's the first day of summer, and none too late. It has been cold and rainy for a full three weeks, which makes it coincidental that the first day of summer falls on the first truly sunny day of June. This morning, the radio forecasts a high temperature of 24 degrees C, and already it's time to take off my sweatshirt.

Yesterday, it cleared off in the late afternoon, and there was extensive blue sky. The DJ on the radio in the early evening told everyone to run outside and look at the moon. It is approaching full, and it's the first time we've been able to see it since new moon. He was right – it did look different sitting there in the clear, darkening sky.

But days are long (the longest today!), and after the moon rose last night, the sky clouded over quicker than I can ever remember anywhere in the past. I was in my kayak, paddling the narrows when the sudden clouding-over began at about 9 PM. I was headed home anyway, and it was a good thing, since the wind started to swirl just as I reached the dock. The grey clouds lowered and broiled, pushing downward in huge cumulus bunches. The grey was mixed with black now, and it was evident this was a significant instability in the local atmosphere. The air was thick with humidity, and the clouds appeared mammatus (normally associated with tornadoes), swirling downward in thrusts of grey bulges. Then the wind hit solidly, unable to establish a steady direction. Large droplets began to fall, and the sky opened suddenly for five minutes of heavy showers. Then, just as quickly as it began, the rain and wind stopped. By midnight, the moon was showing through the clouds again, cruising far south in its summer arc.

\* \* \* \* \*

My mornings often begin with a trip around the float (doesn't take long), hauling in all of the wood that has drifted into my cabin area during the night. Hole in the Wall is exceptionally calm most nights, and driftwood slides in, accumulating in the still water. There is no tide on even the largest fresh water lakes, but there are tidal-like forces here that I never completely understand. Maybe it's caused by changes in the gates at the dam, 10 miles south (down-lake) from here. Or it could just be the natural flow from the Head (20 miles farther up the lake) to the dam. I'm sure the slightest breeze also has something to with the currents, but the flow is not unlike changing tidal currents, just more difficult to predict. Usually, the flow is inwards at night and outward during the day. So I make the early morning driftwood trek around the cabin to prepare for seasons ahead when a wood fire will be needed.

Everyone tries to keep the lake clean, but occasionally junk appears among the driftwood. Included are objects that got away from somebody. Yesterday morning, what looked like a small white wheel and tire floated into the natural swimming pool behind the cabin. In cases like this, I usually ignore the object, and it disappears on its own to clutter someone else's area. But later in the day, I saw the white object again near the kayak dock. This time it was a bit closer, and I immediately noticed it was not a wheel rim and tire but a large white plastic dog dish, floating right-side-up. And there was brown stuff in the bowl. Yes, poor Fido lost his dog dish overboard from his floating cabin during a recent wind, and his favorite dog chow was a victim of the incident. Now my attitude changed. I immediately welcomed the dish aboard, discarded the somewhat aged food, and refilled the bowl with fresh water, awaiting Bro's next visit.

Later today, I plan to crank up my chainsaw for the first time in months. I brought it down from the shed this morning, with the goal of cutting up some of the bigger driftwood so it can be stored in piles. The smaller stuff usually needs attention too, since I store it in bins for kindling. But first, it must be dried. That's a simple process. After a few days on the deck (at least on sunny days), even the most waterlogged wood is ready to burn. I call it "baking" the wood in the sun, so there are always piles of wood stacked everywhere on the deck getting baked. I haul it out of the water wherever I find it, and there it sits for weeks (maybe months) until the chainsaw is buzzing again. If it rains, no harm is done. The wood simply bakes again the next sunny day.

As most people know, a chainsaw in my hands is a sight to behold. Everybody gives me plenty of space when I crank it up. The good news is no one is here today but me, plus usually I can't get the dang thing started anyway. I'm a master at flooding the carburetor all to heck.

Today there is an all-day Beach Boys Endless Summer blast on satellite radio, celebrating the first day of the new season. I grew up with the Beach Boys, and I had forgotten how varied their music is. It is now blaring at full volume – no one else is in the Hole today.

I climb the hill to the outhouse and listen to the blasting music from there. Satellite radio isn't licensed yet in Canada (soon), but my U.S. receiver pulls down the signal just fine. The XM geostationary satellites (officially named "Rock" and "Roll") are low in the sky here, and my antenna barely catches them through a gap in the trees to the south. The slightest obstacle interrupts the signal, so I'm lucky to be on the very edge of coverage. Otherwise I'd have to convince John to top a few trees for me. Neither he nor the forestry folks would take kindly to that.

Satellite radio and telephone technology make a big difference in my comfort level. Satellite phone coverage is fickle, since sky coverage is minimal in the Hole, with granite walls to the north and east, and high trees to the south and west. But I usually receive enough satellites to allow a conversation, sometimes brief, before it dies. Additionally, it gives me a good excuse not to make a lot of phone calls and to receive almost none, since electrical power is from solar panels or (when needed) a small emergency gas generator.

I pulled my floating garden in early this morning and harvested the kind of crop that is a good supplement to my meals. Strawberries, potatoes, and onions are particularly successful this year, although I also cut some asparagus today. Of course, I have no idea how to cook asparagus, but it looked almost store-size, so I couldn't resist.

So here's today's dichotomy – the Beach Boys are blasting away, singing about California surfing and fast cars. Neither is meaningful here. The swells on the nearby Strait of Georgia can be large, especially when the wind is from the southeast, but there are no shallow beaches to produce breaking surf: "If everybody had an ocean, across the USA, then everybody'd be surfin', like Californ-i-ae."

And the only main road through town doesn't go very far. You see few southern California cars here: "Gotta be cool now. Powershift, here we go." The tourists pass through as they race for the ferry: "Pedal to the floor. Hear his two quads drink."

As I write this paragraph, a floatplane cruises up the narrows (directly off my front porch) about 100 feet above the water. He's destined northbound for the Head, probably to drop off logging managers. Like clockwork, I'll expect him buzzing past southbound in another half hour. Sometimes I wave, and he'll rock the wings, if he's looking this way.

The rest of the logging crew shuttles up to the Head at about 6 AM each weekday in an armada of fast and hefty workboats. Sometimes I'm awakened by the gentle rocking of the cabin, when the wakes from the crummy boats reach the float about eight minutes after they pass. It's a barely-noticeable movement that I usually sleep through. It's only the big storms and Lookie-Loos in speedboats within the Hole that really disrupt the float.

I haven't seen any boats in the Hole for days, except for Jess, when he arrived at his float cabin across the bay from me yesterday. He likes to hold conversations on the water. For example, yesterday Jess came into my breakwater with a friend who has purchased a powerful new boat. I noticed that Jess was doing all of the driving, undoubtedly because it's a very nice boat. Although I invited them aboard, they floated about five feet off my deck while we talked for a half hour. Too much work to leave the boat.

When it came time to leave, I asked Jess to give me a demo of the new 175 horse two-stroke. Since the boat is only 18 feet in length, that's plenty of power to cause quite an acceleration from a standing start (two-strokes are known for that). Right off my breakwater entrance, the bow came up high and fast, and the boat dug a deep hole in the water as it accelerated, generating a wake that rocked my float for several minutes afterwards. As they sped away, I watched the owner-passenger holding on for dear life.

The days here just evaporate, partly because any project involving a float cabin is a major project. Just getting stuff to and from the cabin is a project in itself. A few days ago, I offered to help John bring some construction material to his float cabin. John is a true beachcomber and accumulates tons of stuff at all three of his family's cabins. Cabin Number 1 is his normal storage destination. Once construction material gets to his cabin, it stays there until used for something or dragged back to civilization or sometimes dropped (by mistake, of course) into the bowels of the fjord-like lake.

For this particular transport project, we had to load about a dozen sheets of metal roofing into John's truck. It was second-hand material that one of his neighbors was trying to get rid of. Everyone knows John is a collector of everything, so the offers come to him from far and wide.

After struggling to get the roofing material into his truck, we had to drive to the marina, drag the roofing down the dock to his boat and load it. Of course, his boat was already crowded with other stuff, so it took awhile to make room for the metal sheets. When we were done, the sheets of metal were sticking out each side of the rear of the boat by about five feet. Getting out of the marina was a trick in itself.

At John's Number 1 cabin, we unloaded the sheets and then hauled them across a footbridge to shore and then up a steep slope. With so much stored at his cabin, little room remains for more. But you can always climb a bit farther up the slope, so we did so carefully. It's a slippery granite gradient, but we finally got all of the metal sheets in position.

The question, of course, is: What is John going to do with the roofing material? So far, there is no real use, but he's thinking about building a roof over his new sawmill. Of course, he doesn't have the sawmill yet. But he's still thinking about it.

Tomorrow, a similarly involved project is on my schedule. I need to transport my kayak to the marina for mounting on my car-top racks so that I can use it in the ocean. The car is there, the racks are already installed (another John design), but the kayak is here. Towing a kayak is a very slow process, and it rides unstable in-tow if there are any waves at all. So I'm going to try pulling the kayak out of the water tonight and cradling it across the back of the Bayliner for more efficient transport. It's a 22-foot kayak, and the Bayliner's width is only eight feet. Then it goes on top of a 1987 compact Ford Tempo. Use your imagination – it looks a lot like a big yellow banana on a soda cracker.

There's still 12 hours of Beach Boys music to go. ("Catch a wave, and you're sitting on top of the world.") The summer is new, and it won't be endless, but today it seems that way.

# Chapter 12

## Seymour Narrows, Ebbing to Slack

I've always wanted to go across by myself – straight from Powell River to Comox, just like the ferry. It's not exactly uncharted waters, but I have never been alone on such a wide expanse of open water. The goal is similar to flying out-of-sight of land in a single-engine airplane. The first time is a real thrill. All of the subsequent times seem less intense, although the engine always runs auto-rough as soon as the land drops behind.

I pick the perfect day for the Comox crossing, as far as sky conditions are concerned. It's brilliant blue in all quadrants. It is not the perfect day as far as winds are concerned. Strong northwesterlies produce white caps before I pass Harwood Island, but I settle in with the waves. Alone on the command bridge in the mild swells, I realize I still have not learned the rule of securing everything downstairs before every voyage. My personal gear is probably already on the floor of the lower cabin, and I hope that my laptop computer isn't included.

Coming up on my right is a landmark for every ferry crossing – Rebecca Rock (just "Rebecca" to us locals), with tiny "Vivian" in the background. I am now on a trans-shore voyage just like the big guys.

I select a snow-packed peak on Vancouver Island and try to keep the Bayliner pointed toward it. The GPS indicates this heading will keep me tracking toward the Little River ferry dock, but it is easier to point the bow at a peak than to watch the glare of the GPS screen in the bright sunlight.

Every time I allow my attention to divert to the rhythm of the waves, I find my bow pointed to the left of the peak as I am pushed south by the waves. Correcting to the right continually, I follow an arcing path that is a lot less efficient than the straight route of the ferry. I am homing in an arc toward the peak rather than properly tracking in a straight line.

Waves pound the Bayliner, but her captain is well below his safety threshold in 3-foot seas. The same waves in the past on Powell Lake (it's rare to get 3-foot waves there) seem death-defying in the Campion. It isn't only the difference in boat size and design (no bowriders on the ocean, please). Over time, I am actually becoming more experienced and less frightened by the sea. In fact, waves that I remember as huge in the past were probably smaller than these three-footers. Time teaches, and time heals. But time also sows dangerous complacency.

Halfway to Comox, I find myself thinking about deadheads – logs that have sunk below the water. Sometimes they are visible to an eagle eye (which excludes me), as they ride right below the waterline. Often the submerged logs float vertically in the water, with the primary profile of the hazard out of sight. Deadheads are hidden icebergs of disaster that may be totally invisible, as was the case recently for the editor of a boating magazine. The deadhead destroyed the editor's entire engine leg and prop with absolutely no warning. Deadheads can float a few inches below the surface, in prop territory, and they are easily hidden in large troughs – in troughs like these.

Approaching the Comox ferry terminal at Little River (more appropriately, arcing toward Little River like a lame duck), the waves begin to ease. I make the turn northward along the shore, passing abeam the *Queen of Burnaby* nestled in her dock. I gaze at the ferry, realizing that the her captain is probably looking forward to the thrill of his next crossing to Powell River with an is-that-all-there-is attitude. I have accomplished my goal, but the ferry captain is probably bored stiff by this route, as he dreams of a real trans-oceanic voyage.

I have attempted to time my departure to make it through Seymour Narrows north of Campbell River at slack tide, but that is now out of the question. A late start, an arcing course, and slow progress in the headwinds and waves have put me behind schedule. I will not make my ultimate goal for this trip (Octopus Islands) tonight.

I refuel at Campbell River and launch for my revised destination of Gowlland Harbour. I am tired of fighting the waves, so the nearby sheltered waters of Gowlland are met with weary enthusiasm.

It is a tranquil cove that absorbs me as I anchor in the back-bay near an extensive log boom and just out of way of the boat traffic taking the shortcut to the adjacent tourist resort at April Point. As I settle in, a recreational crab fisherman drops his traps nearby, and we talk boat-to-boat about his traps. The fisherman notes that none of the election returns are in yet, but he promises to let me know the preliminary results when he retrieves his traps in a few hours. I didn't realize it is election day, and I prefer not to confess my nationality at the moment, so I simply thank him. I am asleep in the V-berth when he returns (probably near the near the end of summer twilight), and that is for the best. I know even less of what happens in Canadian politics than most residents of BC who often remind me: "We're a long way from Ottawa." I drop off to sleep thinking about my morning departure for the turn of the tide at Seymour Narrows.

I've witnessed substantial tidal flows in years past. Margy and I rode the current at Dodd Narrows in our kayak, an exciting interlude to a sleepy camping trip in the Gulf Islands. It wasn't even close to maximum current, but it was enough to create significant swirls and several major whirlpools. The brief ride through that channel was exhilarating, and I remember screaming with joy the entire way, paddling more frantically than necessary to keep the kayak on course. Margy, on the other hand, was simultaneously screaming with fright. She resolved never to ride through a whirlpool area in a kayak again.

I purposefully avoided the current at Malibu Rapids during a trip to Chatterbox Falls with John, timing our arrival to enter the rapids at slack tide. There was a line of waiting boats when we arrived at the rapids, each announcing their queued lineup on Channel 16. John felt it was "stupid" – he wanted to run the rapids before the tide turned, jumping ahead of the waiting boats. I knew he was just trying to aggravate me (successfully), since John would never be so inconsiderate. But he wanted it clear there was no danger in these rapids for an accomplished boater. In fact, he loves the challenge of tidal currents. By the time we made it through (last in line), Malibu Rapids was a big letdown for both of us.

I've walked the path to Skookumchuck with John, watching rough-water kayaks ride the huge standing waves in 12-knot swirls, and I've seen the flowing white water between islands from an airplane (if it looks that savage from the air…).

I watch as John docks at Egmont when Skookumchuck is starting to flood. It's the only time I've seen John make two passes at a dock (after a go-around). When I finally throw the young fuel attendant a rope, I kid the teenager: "He's just a student pilot. I'm his instructor." John glares at me with a look that could kill.

Now, thinking about Seymour Narrows as I drift off to sleep, it should not be a big deal. I know as much about rapids as the next guy, and my boat's size is adequate for a few knots of flow. Nevertheless, I barely sleep at Gowlland that night, thinking about the Narrows and constantly awakening and recomputing the timing of my departure – add 1 hour to the tide tables for daylight savings time, subtract 30 minutes for travel time from here, and subtract 30 more minutes for hoisting anchor and preparing the boat. It is like counting sheep in reverse.

I decide I will leave a bit early in the morning to assure I arrive at the Narrows before slack water. I can wait at the entrance or, if brave enough, start into the Narrows early to experience a bit of rapids. It is like my first solo cross-country flight. I am both excited and apprehensive. On the satellite phone earlier in the evening, John suggests I try a significant taste of rapids. His method of teaching by trial-and-error always develops my skills and will either make a man out of me or scare me all to hell.

I hoist anchor in the morning, well before the appointed time. The winds are fairly strong from the northwest, so I may have to proceed slowly to the Narrows under these conditions. Once out in the open channel, the winds are less than advertised, so I make good time. The tidal flow is now northward (into the narrows from my present position), but in less than an hour it will switch to its flooding southward movement. My plan is to be in place at slack tide, maybe entering the Narrows a few minutes before the tide turns, to take advantage of the push northward.

As I approach Seymour Narrows, two commercial tugs are exiting the passage as the ebbing tide approaches slack. Both vessels (with nothing in-tow) have pushed through on the ebbing tide, uphill. It is 30 minutes before slack, and the passage ahead looks smooth. I push the throttle forward and venture into the gap. Tidal swirls and rip currents boil everywhere, but the passage is as uneventful as I had hoped. The biggest scare occurs when a sport fishing boat passes me in a quick spurt, scaring me momentarily as it suddenly appears off my right side. He probably wonders why a 25-knot boat is putzing through these waters at only 10 knots.

The waters smooth in about a mile, giving way to wind waves on the west side of Quadra Island. Similar to the previous day, the waves are safe but pounding. My progress is slow, although creeping closer to shore reduces the wave heights a bit. By the time I reach the northwest corner of Quadra, I am ready for a rest, but there is no taking a break in these waters. Kanish Bay invites me, although it is well short of my destination of the Octopus Islands. I accept the invitation, pull out of the waves, and within minutes am in the large, nearly calm bay. Except for fish farms, there is little activity as I head toward the rear of the bay and a small inlet, Granite Bay.

Entering this tiny bay is a trip back in time. Old boats, many no longer serviceable, are moored or tied to a small dock. The ruins of the old public wharf are dangling disconnected from the shoreline now, a remnant of the busy days of the early 1900s when Granite Bay was a thriving community of over 500 people. None of the boats in the bay seem active, so I drop a short-rode anchor, less than the recommended ratio of anchor rope to depth for real holding-power. I bob in the center of the bay on a lunch hook. But I am more in the mood for a nap than lunch. I slip my flat-iron shaped satellite radio antenna through the V-berth hatch onto the foredeck, tune in CNBC, and let the stock market report lull me to sleep. I am listening for the Dow average, but before I hear it, I am sound asleep.

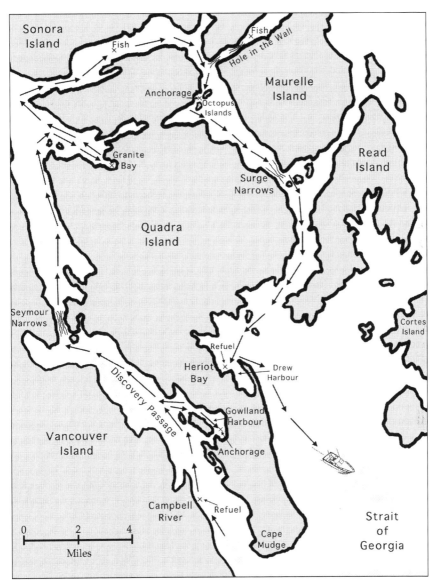

I am out of Kanish Bay by 2 PM, after a brief delay to dislodge the anchor from the muddy bottom. John is holding the foot-switch of my anchor winch hostage in his garage. The switch has become another victim of the harsh saltwater environment, but John will eventually repair it. For now, I'm forced to manually sweat my way through the hoisting of the anchor. Two thick anchor winch wires dangle from the roof of the V-berth. ("Now, Wayne, don't touch those wires together, whatever you do," said John on the satellite phone the previous night.) Pulling the small anchor by hand is not difficult, but the winch would be handy for this mud-lodged situation. I fiddle with the anchor awhile, and then use a burst of reverse throttle to dislodge it. In the process, I swear a few words regarding John. He deserves no swear words (ever), but a few in a situation like this, just for good measure, seems fair.

As I leave Kanish Bay, the waves in the channel are a pleasant surprise – they are substantially reduced. Conditions continue to improve, and by the time I round the northwest corner of Quadra, the sea is smooth. I stop once over a center-channel reef to fish (nothing), and then press on toward the Octopus Islands on the northeast corner of Quadra.

But there is one more stop on my agenda. By coincidence rather than planning, slack tide is about to occur at the west end of the other Hole in the Wall, the Hole that boaters in this area respect. It's a narrow entrance with mountain walls on each side, opening to a wider channel beyond. The tidal currents here are infamous.

Approaching Hole in the Wall, the sea boils in small whirlpools, although slack tide is only minutes away. I enter the west entrance as the flood tide finishes its dominance, providing a slight uphill fight going in. But the entrance is easily navigated in the Bayliner. Several kayaks followed me in.

Once inside, the Hole opens wider, revealing a beautiful landscape, but not as beautiful as my own Hole in the Wall. The mountains are higher than home, but they are gentle slopes rather than nearly-vertical faces.

I fish (without success) in the center of the channel, waiting for the exact moment of slack tide. That moment comes and goes without any change in the minor swirling around me, and after a few minutes of further fishing (still nothing), I retreat back through the entrance, pushing against the swirls with no problem. It is only a mile from this entrance to the Octopus Islands, making it hard to believe that this massive tidal upset will not affect those islands. It doesn't.

Entering the Octopus Islands through narrow Tentacle Passage, I find ample space for anchoring, although it is already late June.

There is an amazing difference between late June and the turn of the people tide in early July.

I select the largest bay, and join two other boats in a cove that will hold at least 15 in another week. I can remember sitting on the cafe deck at Squirrel Cove (Cortes Island) the previous year on an equally sunny day, the first day of July (Canada Day), wondering where all of the crowds were hiding. Only a handful of boats were anchored in Squirrel Cove that day, and I was the lone patron of the cafe. A week later, Squirrel Cove would be crowded with over 50 boats. It's from peace to (relative) chaos in the span of a week. June is a superb month for boating in British Columbia, but it's July and August that attract the deluge of boats, flooding north in July and ebbing southward (homeward) in August and early September.

The next morning, I am prepared for one more set of rapids. Surge Narrows will record its low tide at 10:48 AM. Now be careful with the math – 9:35 is low tide at Point Atkinson, plus 13 minutes for displacement to Surge Narrows, plus 1 hour to convert to daylight savings time, and don't forget travel time from here to there. But I sleep well in the Octopus Islands. I don't count sheep or tide tables, and I am wide-awake and waiting for my self-declared engine-start time (10:00).

As I wait, I watch birds on the shoreline. Most are foraging, as the approaching low tide reveals added real estate. Then I do a double-take – a huge bald eagle is in the middle of a group of crows. Look again – there is another bald eagle about 100 feet farther down the shoreline, with its own squadron of crows.

I think of eagles as the terrorists of the bird world. I've watched them swoop down for fish, and I am surprised to see crows pecking the rocks nearby, as if the eagles are merely other crows. By size alone, these eagles are not crows. At this close range, they are larger than I expect, beefy brown birds with the traditional white neck and head, and that unmistakable sharp beak and determined face. I am the closest I have ever been to a bald eagle, although they are a common sight along this part of the coast. But I have never previously seen them simply standing on the shoreline.

The crows walk and peck. The two eagles stand nearly motionless, moving their heads slowly to inspect for shoreline food. By comparison, the crows' walk-and-peck motions seem inefficient. How much easier it is to rotate your head slowly, taking in all of your surroundings with your eagle eyes. I expect the eagles to attack the crows, but they don't. (I later learn the reverse is often true – crows and ravens are known to harass eagles.)

Inspecting closer with my binoculars, I notice that the crows give the eagles a few feet clearance at all times. And when the first bald eagle finally decides to leave, all of the crows immediately scatter. When the eagle takes flight, it is sudden and dramatic. He pushes quickly off the shore, wings spread to nearly six feet, as he swoops low across the Octopus Islands with long, slow wing strokes. His partner seems to ignore his leaving, the crows reappear in a few minutes, and then all is interrupted again by the second eagle's departure. (Okay, now that you're all back, I'll just depart and stress you out again.)

I exit the Octopus Islands slowly through the east entrance, a route that is best navigated, as it is today, at low tide, when you can see the rocks and reefs. Once in the open channel, it is smooth water all the way to Surge Narrows.

I am nearly a half-hour early, so I consider waiting for slack water. That thought is reinforced by the narrow opening (Beazley Passage) that makes it difficult to see boats coming the other way. It would not be courteous to transit southeastbound (as I am about to do) before the tide turns to flood, since an opposing boat might be traveling through on the final minutes of the ebbing tide. But I approach close enough to the swirling water to see all of the way through the passage. It is empty, and I am ready. So I go.

It is a fantastic ride, not quite as violent as Dodd Narrows in the kayak, but definitely an invigorating ride. And it is downhill, which doesn't make sense. It is not yet slack water (should be ebbing to slack), so the flow is in the wrong direction. It seems I have obviously miscomputed the tide, but I can't figure it out even later with an after-the-fact review of the Canadian tide tables.

As I exit the rapids, there are plenty of small whirlpools to play in, so I loiter. I place the throttle in idle and let the boat drift wherever it wants to go. It wants to go every-which-way. Then I apply power and experiment with my control over the boat. The exercise is safe

and controlled, providing me applied experience regarding the in-
fluence of the currents, and I pack this knowledge away for future
rapids. John would be proud of me.

I turn back to face the passage and watch a commercial barge
power its way out of the passage (no problem). As I start to turn
away from the rapids, the corner of my eye notices a yellow kayak
swirling in the lower tidal flow. The kayak is empty, and it is going
down fast in a whirlpool. The barge also sees the kayak and reverses course immediately. I am farther away from the kayak than
the barge is, and I am glad he is here. A lost kayak (if recovered) will
require a report and towing, but the barge can simply scoop up the
kayak and take it along as the captain simultaneously reports the
incident to the Coast Guard.

Wait a minute – the kayak is not empty. I see the legs of a dog
kicking out of one end of the kayak. Wait, the dog is wearing a
red life vest. No, the dog is a human being, struggling to right the
kayak and bail the water from it. It seems a hopeless cause, as the
kayak continues to swirl, bow under water (or is it the stern). Now it
is nearly level again, but with a very low waterline (but improving).
The kayaker waves his paddle to the barge, and a barge crewmember
yells back: "Got her, do ya?!"

All settles down in a few minutes. The kayak, now mostly bailed,
turns and exits to the northeast. I note that the drenched paddler is
a small woman, not even close to a dog. The barge reverses course
again and chugs toward the south. I sit and watch the white water
roiling out of the passage for a few more minutes. Then I follow the
barge, passing it within a few miles.

After refueling (boat and human) at Heriot Bay on southeastern
Quadra Island, I depart the dock before the ferry arrives. That's a
good decision – at low tide, the small bay is a bit constricted. I will
regroup and begin to stow my gear in Drew Harbour, immediately
adjacent to Heriot Bay. This is my last leg home, and I'd like to arrive in Westview and put my boat to bed as quickly as possible. It
will be hot at home, although it is island-cool here.

I pull into the entrance of Drew Harbour and cut the engine.
No anchor will be needed for a short visit here. I'm just in time to
watch the arrival of the Cortes Island ferry as it slips into nearby

Heriot Bay. The Bayliner bobs up and down in its wake, as I deploy the flat-iron satellite radio antenna one more time to catch the closing bell. (Always a stock fanatic, today is interest rate decision-day for the U.S. Federal Reserve – the Fed raises the rate by a quarter point.) I turn up the volume so I can hear the radio as I stow the anchor rode that has been drying on the deck. I tidy up the cabin and pack my clothes and the numerous books I always lug from place to place. A variety of battery-powered lanterns are returned to their storage locations. I remind myself to buy more batteries – I always feel more confident when I have a full-year's supply.

I have been on this boat continuously for 48 hours, except for two brief refueling stops. That is not a long time aboard a boat, but this is a small boat. I could have gone to shore by dinghy at either of my overnight stops, but it wasn't necessary. I am happy here, the lone inhabitant of a craft that nurtures me. I love her small spaces, the cramped cabinets, and the narrow cabin passageway. I feel my way around at night. During the day, I know the touch of the handholds and footholds from the stern to the foredeck, around the outside of the cabin. I am a monkey, climbing up and down, over and around.

Now the cabin is secure, and all is ready for the last leg of this journey. I stow the satellite antenna and exit Drew Harbour, requiring a northeasterly course to safely clear the tip of the spit. The channel is as smooth as the sea ever gets. I glance at the small triangle that marks my GPS position and I zoom out on the screen to view the route home to Westview. The track needed to exit the harbor is almost exactly 050 degrees, and a turn 60 degrees farther to the right after clearing the spit will put me right on course, a straight shot to my destination. So that equates to a no-wind heading of 110 degrees.

I clear the spit and slowly push the throttle forward, rise up on-plane, trim the bow upward, and turn right to 110 degrees. I glance at the GPS again, and it now looks like 120 degrees is what is needed. I make a slight correction to the right, and my nose is pointed at the tip of an island in the distance. The visibility is over 50 miles, so that might be Savary Island on the nose. In a few miles,

I check my position again. It is now apparent it is not Savary that I see. I am looking all the way to Texada Island, and I am looking at the northwest tip. Thus, it's back to the left by 10 degrees. My original heading of 110 was correct, after all.

Cruising contentedly on-plane, I let out a "Yahoo!" No one hears, so I do it again. There are no boats in sight in any direction, and I am lonely in a very wonderful way. "Yahoo!" makes the sea even smoother.

There is a sudden surge in the engine, a throaty noise accompanied by a sudden loss of thrust. This is the third time I have heard it on this trip but the first time at cruise power (the other instances were during acceleration). Each previous time, the sound and feel were so subtle I was not certain whether it was an engine sound or the change of the position of the earflaps of my safari cap. Maybe it was a mere sound perception. But not this time – it is a surging, throaty sound, and it goes away when I reduce power to idle and re-accelerate. I'm confident that I will make it home safely, but John's attention to this problem will be needed.

Back on-plane again, the tip of Texada dominates the horizon in front of me. The island's tip is shaped like an elephant landmark I know in California. Near Mojave, there is a mountain that (from the air) looks like an elephant lying down, its trunk stretched out far forward. That is how Texada looks from here, a crouching elephant that is an hour away at my cruising speed of 23 knots.

My hands are off the wheel. Everything is in perfect trim, and the ocean is flat. I see an occasional object on the horizon ahead, maybe floaters in my eyes, maybe birds, maybe distant boats. They come and go. Some are birds. Straight ahead is a flock of KMAs, and I decide to go around them. Even on my revised route, my boat disturbs the ducks even before I pass. All but one dive under water, their duck butts the last to go, reminding me of their nickname (kiss-my-ass). One KMA remains, and I pass 20 feet abeam as he too dives (ducks) underwater.

My course is straight and smooth. Hernando Island is passing off my left, and I check the GPS again in zoom-out mode. Mystery Reef is nearly directly ahead. I have always wanted to fish there,

and I will do so today, as a final stop en route home. The reason I
have never fished Mystery Reef previously is that it is so far from
land. Today, I will arrive there comfortably from the seaward side.
Perspectives change with time and experience.

Directly in my path, there is a dark object about 200 feet ahead.
This is no floater in my eye, nor is it a bird or a boat. It is a whale.
The tail of the giant beast is displayed in perfect profile as the whale
dives beneath the waves. It is now below the water directly ahead,
so I hold my course, hoping the whale will resurface in this same
area. Within less than a minute, I am at its diving point. No whale,
but I may have passed directly over it, so it might resurface behind
me. I turn and stare rearward. The wake of my boat is powerful
and beautiful. It stretches straight. There is no further evidence of
the whale. But I continue looking back at my spreading wake. In the
distance is Quadra Island. Back there, but never to be forgotten.

\* \* \* \* \*

After arriving home, I drive to John's house and explain my engine
surge observations. It is my perception that the stern-drive leg is
kicking up or the exhaust port suddenly pops above the water's sur-

face. John says the leg cannot kick up under the force of the propeller (except in reverse thrust). He says it might be a blown prop seal. That means nothing to me.

I walk with John to his shed, he reaches onto a shelf, and retrieves a prop with a blown seal. What is the chance that a person would have a blown prop in their shed? John has a full demo model.

The next day we take the Bayliner through a dramatic series of steep turns and accelerations and decelerations. John hauls the boat around with rough precision. On the aft deck, Bro is hanging on for dear life. We duplicate the problem, and John no longer thinks it is a blown prop. Upon returning to the dock, we tilt the leg upward and find a tiny stick lodged in the edge of the anti-cavitation fin. It is enough to disturb the flow around the prop (it doesn't take much), so John removes the stick and out we go for another test run. ("Hang on, Bro!" yells John.) The problem is solved. I tell John the local boat shop would have solved the problem equally well – by replacing the entire leg. Removing a stick is a lot cheaper.

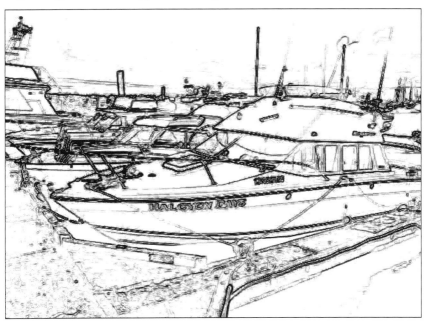

◊ ◊ ◊ ◊ ◊ ◊ ◊

# Chapter 13

## The Smell of Elk

We drive north from Duck Lake, with John's 660cc Grizzly in the bed of the truck and my 420cc Kodiak on the trailer behind us. The metal loading ramps rattle around in back, slapping within the bed of the truck and squeaking in concert with the bumps in the dirt road. John's power steering has been out for the past few miles, and he is working hard to keep the truck aimed correctly.

"Must be the pump," he says. "I've been adding fluid for several weeks. Can't see where the fluid's going."

John comes to a halt, quick enough to cause the loading ramps to shift again and whack against the back of the cab. A family of grouse is strolling down the edge of the road, a mamma and three babies. Bro sees the birds but chooses to ignore them. There are bigger animals to howl at in these woods. We start to roll again, John still fighting the steering wheel.

We are barely rolling after the stop for the grouse when a deer pokes her head out of the bush on the right side of the road. Bro decides this is what he's looking for, and starts his howling siren at full throttle.

The deer crosses the road slowly, seemingly not frightened by the approaching truck (probably doesn't know that John's steering is out) or the dog's ugly, loud howl. Bro shifts his body to the driver's side, climbing over John and clambering against the side window. John rolls down the window, and Bro nearly leaps out of the vehicle, his head following the bushes where the doe exits the road to the left. A half-mile farther down the road, Bro's howling finally stops. He licks his chops, and settles back down, still draped over John.

"Do you mind?" says John. Bro doesn't mind. He's content to continue the ride spread out over the John's lap, so that's where he stays. Now John has a monster truck without power steer and a rotund Labrador Retriever in his lap.

"All we need around the next bend is a bear," remarks John. Fortunately for all of us, there is no bear.

We park in a turnout to the left, unload our quads, and get ready to ride.

\* \* \* \* \*

**A**s we approach a bridge on the logging road, there are six quads on the left shoulder, along with a smoldering campfire. This is the bridge that is scheduled for removal any day now, and an alternate quad trail is already under construction.

We park our quads and walk across the bridge. Metal tire-path slabs emblazoned with sloppily painted white "X" marks indicate the fate of this structure. I guess it would be bad if the road crew took out the wrong bridge.

On the other side of the creek, a well-groomed trail leads upstream, with two riders (workers today) filling dirt in the trench that borders the road. The trench separating the road from the trail will be steep, but easily navigated by a quad.

As we discuss the progress of the new trail with the riders, a brown pickup truck pulls up, stops, and the young bearded driver asks how soon we think the bridge will be demolished.

"We hear it will be gone within a week," says one of the riders.

"I expect it to disappear any day now," notes the truck driver. "I'm cutting shakes near the head of the lake, so it looks like I will be out of work here pretty soon."

"Got any good cedar?" asks John.

"It's for the taking now," says the truck driver. "I won't be able to get many more shake blocks out before this bridge is gone, so you're welcome to it."

John's eyes light up, but we'd have no way to extract the kind of logs John is looking for. It's mostly sections of trees, good enough for an independent shake blocker like the bearded fellow, but not the large logs John needs for a new float. Even if the logs were here, how could we get them out?

"Wish I could use your trail," says the shake blocker. "That would solve everything."

"Have at it," says John.

The bearded man laughs. There's no way his truck could make it through the narrow path. It's a nice trail, wide enough for a quad, but much too brutal for a pickup truck.

We walk up the new trail. This portion, now complete, is landscaped with logs and rocks off to the sides. The trail leads to a new wooden bridge over the creek about 200 feet up the ravine. Two hefty logs are already in place to support the split cedar logs that will form the base of the wooden bridge. It's wide enough for a quad. Two workers are finishing up the approach to the bridge on this side, using shovels and picks to smooth the final turn.

"You selected this specific location for a reason," I note to one of the workers.

"It's a nice narrow spot in the stream and seems to be a place where there is little washout activity," he says. "And we want it as close to the road as possible to save work on the trail construction."

"Nice job," says John. His words are appreciated by a group that knows trail construction well and respects John's knowledge.

"You might consider taking out that tree on the other side," notes John. He points to a small tree that is slightly to the left of the exit path on the other end of the bridge. "It would make the turn back onto the trail on the other side a lot easier."

"You're right, it is a bit in the way, isn't it?" says the worker.

I can see it too, now that John has mentioned it. As you leave the bridge, the curve will be difficult to negotiate on a quad.

But I bet the tree stays.

* * * * *

We start our quads, cross the soon-to-be-gone logging bridge, and drive only a few hundred feet before we find three more quads parked to the side of the road.

"This is where they're cutting the wood for the bridge," says John. "They use cedar logs discarded by the loggers, splitting the wood with wedges to make the boards."

We trudge up the hill over fallen logs and John introduce me to two men who are working on a 5-foot section of cedar log. They hammer wedges into the grain of the wood until it splits in nice long sections.

"Too many knots," says one of the workers. "Knots make it impossible to split."

Cedar is the wood of choice, since it is easy to split and slow to rot. Cedar is the only respectable wood to use for a float and the deck of a cabin. Bridges too.

Another worker is farther up the hill, nearly out of sight. He has found some knotless cedar, although it is a long drag back to the road. But it turns out to be the necessary solution.

The entire trail building process is a marvel to watch from the outside looking in. Everyone seems to have a specialty, and each man is working with a small team to construct the trail. It seems like no one is in charge. It just happens, sort of like the work of an ant colony. In reality, this is pretty much how the trail progresses, but it works only because the friends know each other well and what to expect from each other's area of expertise. The end product is closer to a national park trail than an alternate route around a soon-to-be-eliminated bridge.

✷ ✷ ✷ ✷ ✷

Back on the logging road, we round the curve at a slash, and John pulls over to the side of the road. He gets off his bike as I pull up behind him.

"Smell the elk?" asks John, as he walks to the edge of the roadside and peers into the slash below. His head and nose are noticeably raised and sniffing.

"What do elk smell like?" I ask.

"Like a barnyard," is his simple reply.

I try real hard, and I think I can smell the elk. But it could be my imagination.

We don't see any elk, but John knows they are here. As we progress farther up the road, he rides slowly, nose upturned, sniffing for elk. It looks like Bro is smelling for them too.

We are trying to reach a newly constructed logging road. John wants to show me the forest that will soon be decimated. Some of the grandest trees lie along the side of new logging roads, but not for long.

Only a mile from the new road, our path is blocked by a logging operation in progress. We come to a stop. Ahead of us giant excavators are being used as cranes to move recently cut logs. The cranes and logs block the road completely. One crane is sorting logs, moving them into neat piles beside the road. Another crane is in the middle of the road, loading logs onto a truck. It is the furthest crane from us, and from this distance, the logs hoisted by the crane look like long toothpicks. The crane picks up logs without visible effort. Hydraulics and huge steel structures do all of the work.

"Hear the helicopter?" asks John.

I remove my helmet and listen. In the background, beyond the noise of the cranes, I hear a helicopter.

"They're probably hauling shakes," says John. "We can't go any farther, so let's head back to the lake to see if we can get a view of the chopper."

We reverse course, drive about a mile back down the road, and turn off onto a trail that leads to a spot near the head of Haslam

Lake. We stop at the lake for lunch and watch a helicopter fly to a shake block site over the ridge beyond the opposite side of the lake. The helicopter comes over the ridge with the shakes trailing below on a long cable. Then the chopper quickly descends to a logging road near the edge of the lake and drops the blocks near the await-ing logging truck. Every five minutes, a circuit is completed; back up over the ridge to pick up more shake blocks and then rapidly down to the lake again.

"That's gotta be expensive," says John. "Usually they extract the shakes a lot closer to the drop site. It's hard to believe they can make money in an operation like that, with helicopter time so expensive."

Helicopter logging is especially expensive and outrageously dangerous. The load on the helicopter as the pile of shakes is lifted would be disastrous if the chopper's engine even hiccups during the pickup. There would be no time to recover for an autorotation emergency landing. And the surrounding forest is not exactly the ideal crash landing site.

"Hear that?" asks John. It is what John does not hear that draws his attention. The background noise of the cranes has stopped. Maybe they are done for the day. If so, we should be able to get through to the new logging road.

By the time we leave the lake and get back to the spot where the cranes were working, the way is clear. We pass the giant Hitachi cranes on the side of the road, drive through thick bark and log remnants, and continue up the road another mile to the start of the new logging road. It's a brand new road, with only a few tire treads in soft dirt. Deep drop-offs border the road, leading to drainage ditches that seem much larger than necessary. If a logging truck goes off the road, it will be a major mess. If we go off the road, it will be a minor personal mess.

We cruise the new road, right tires in the wide tread mark and left tires on the center median of dirt. We weave through sections of second-growth timber, tall and beautiful. It's hard to imagine that these huge trees have grown since the original logging of this area in the early 1900s. There is no old-growth in this area, since all of it was cut nearly a hundred years ago. Imagine what this forest would look like covered by trees with trunks over twice the diameter of these giants.

Building these roads is a marvel in itself. They may only be dirt, but you still have to thrust them through the forest. Loggers cut the initial path, and the heavy excavating equipment comes behind with the necessary brute force. It is a road with only one purpose – getting loggers to the trees in order to cut them down and speed the wood to the mill.

The new road section has cutoff our old quad trail to Giovanni Lake. We stop where the road cuts through that trail.

"They used the quad trail as part of the route for the new road," says John. He points to the entry path to Giovanni that I drove with him the previous year. The trail is now cutoff by a trench and a small logging slash along the side of the new road.

"We can fix it, though it'll take some work," says John.

The new road suddenly ends, and we are back on a road I've driven previously. It winds down to Powell Lake. We take a break at the shoreline, sitting on a granite precipice, gazing northward out over one of the world's most gorgeous lakes. Goat Island is on the opposite side, and the jagged peaks topped by glaciers are to our right, towards Goat Lake. The sky is blue with puffy cumulus in a warm summer sun. A trout darts out from the shore in front of us, disturbed by two human beings and a dog.

\* \* \* \* \*

John leads me back to his truck on a route through Fiddlehead Farm. It's a bit farther this way, but it provides a change of scenery. Within a half-hour, we are back at the soon-to-be-gone bridge and the new trail. We pull onto the trail to try the new wooden bridge. We are the first customers.

The work crew has already departed, and the trail is complete. As we approach the bridge, John orders us to a stop to survey the wooden structure.

"They sure did a good job," he says.

That they did. It's a work of art, the wooden planks looking smooth and refined, after hours of grunt work.

I look across to the opposite shore, and the tree that John suggested removing is gone. The corner on that side of the bridge is now clear of obstacles.

"They took out the tree," says John with obvious pride.

I never had any doubt.

# Chapter 14

## Maksutov-Cassegrain in the Kitchen

Noise travels a long way over quiet water. It is after midnight, and I hesitate before punching the Go-To button on my telescope. The only occupants in the Hole tonight are Jess and me, and he is probably asleep in his cabin on the other side of the bay. My telescope clattered through the alignment process an hour ago, but now is the appointed time to push the Go-To button and see if M31, the Andromeda Galaxy, is ready for scrutiny. The galaxy has arisen above Goat and is ready for viewing, but the telescope's alignment may have gone astray, depending on how far the float has drifted. If it's not in the eyepiece, I may be able to fine-tune things without a complete realignment. Otherwise, I'll have to go through the noisy realignment process. Noisy? It's really only a few finely-meshed gears rotating at a very slow speed. Not exactly a chainsaw. But I bet Jess hears it on his float on this calm (i.e., quiet) night. If he hears it, Jess will surely wonder what's going on. What is the American doing now?

I push the button, and the small telescope swings toward the east, slows after a few seconds (quieter now), as the low-speed gears begin to slue. The faint gear noise stops, there is a beep (seems loud!) to tell me the telescope thinks it is pointing at the object, and all is perfectly quiet again. In the city, the loudest gears and the beep would be totally unnoticeable from the house next door, and that house is a lot closer than Jess' cabin. Of course, in the city, you wouldn't be able to see the Andromeda Galaxy.

I'm not sure why I am so nervous about the murmur of the telescope. Jess already thinks I'm a crazy American, and the grinding of gears in the middle of the night will only further reinforce that image. It's so damn quiet here. Now the deck is creaking as I walk in my bare feet. Besides the grinding gear noises and the electronic beep, the American walks around his deck all night long.

I do walk around the deck nearly all night long on nights like this. The sky is overwhelming through a small telescope in the Hole. This particular instrument has less than half the light-gathering mirror area of my larger telescope in California. In the dark southern California desert, there is a remote airport called Desert Center where I take that larger Schmidt-Cassegrain scope on clear nights. I fly in (I have never seen another airplane there), set up my tent, and wait for the desert darkness. That Cassegrain produces about the same results there as this tiny (by comparison) telescope produces on my float.

This telescope is of Maksutov-Cassegrain design, similar to my larger scope, and I am amazed how powerful it acts in the dark skies of the Hole in the Wall. It is not just the darkness, although that is important. Astronomers compare observing conditions by noting the transparency (clarity of the sky) and the seeing (steadiness of the image). Here in the Hole, light pollution is almost non-existent, with Powell River's glow barely distinguishable to the south. Transparency is usually outstanding on clear nights, and seeing is miraculously steady. The clear skies are evident in some interesting and indirect ways. Dust simply does not accumulate. The normal city-like film of dust that you'd expect on objects in the cabin is nonexistent. Even when the cabin is open and fully operational, no dust accumulates – absolutely none. It is a strange (and wonderful) circumstance that makes you realize how extremely clean the air is. It's a joy for housekeeping too.

The seeing was my biggest surprise. I now attribute the fine seeing to the stability caused by the water surface at night. The water is usually cooler than the air, inviting a very stable lower atmosphere. I've read about naked-eye observers who discovered they can see fainter stars from boats because of this condition. Unfortunately, boats are not conducive to the lack of motion required by telescopes. Even binoculars are rather worthless as sky tools from a boat, with newer, stabilized binoculars being the exception.

Thus, when I first look through a telescope in the Hole, I wonder what havoc a floating cabin will have on my observations. Not only will movement of any kind upset the telescopic image, it could also cause loss of an object after a very brief period of high-magnificaton, making the operational principles of a modern Go-To telescope nearly worthless. I don't hope for much. I receive plenty.

Clear nights are usually calm nights, so the float experiences minimal movement during such observing sessions. In any conditions short of rough waves and strong winds, you don't perceive the movement of the float at all. Small float movements in moderate winds can be detected, if you really pay attention, but only the strongest winds and waves cause motion that is enough to be really noticeable. One of the unique things about living on a float is what happens when you go ashore after several days of float life – everything seems to move around a little bit for the first few hours on shore.

But a passing boat sets the float to rocking, even with the protection of the log breakwater. So even if it is a calm night, a boat in the channel could cause float movement and upset the telescope's Go-To alignment. The good news is that there are no boats in the channel late at night. Problem solved.

There is no way to see if the float will make a good telescope foundation without testing it. I expect the test to show that such an observational platform is nearly useless. So on the first test of the new telescope, I am not surprised when nothing seems to work properly. Either that, or the telescope's Go-To mechanism is seriously malfunctioning. After aligning the telescope, the very first Go-To object is a miss by several degrees, placing it barely inside the finder scope's field of view and completely outside even the lowest power eyepiece. The next Go-To object is completely beyond the finder's wide field of view. In other words, things start out bad and get rapidly worse.

Modern amateur telescopes incorporate Go-To tracking technology that was unheard of 20 years ago, except in the world's largest telescopes. Go-To technology allows an observer to select an object in the computer database, direct the telescope to a precise location, and then track the object as it moves across the sky. Even 10 years ago, this technology was still too expensive to reach the lower amateur astronomer ranks. Today, Go-To tracking is commonplace, extremely accurate, and amazingly inexpensive. Just don't try it on the deck of a floating home.

Or have I encountered a factory-defective telescope alignment system? I know it can't be a slightly defective system, since these errors are major.

One day, when John is on our float, I demonstrate the power of the telescope's optics to him. He focuses the telescope on Goat, and scans the island with excitement. He appreciates quality technology. I explain the alignment problems I am experiencing (impossible to duplicate during the daytime) and he seems to comprehend exactly how the Go-To mechanism works. There is an alignment test that can be conducted during the daytime on land objects, but the float is moving around a lot as daytime boats in the channel send out their upsetting wakes. The terrestrial test is a non-surprising failure under these conditions, but John thinks about it further, and feels it is really the telescope and not the float that is primarily at fault. He doesn't completely understand the alignment process (not a telescope expert, not a computer expert, and not a Go-To enthusiast), but he feels that a factory adjustment is necessary.

Easier said than done. The factory is in California. Long distance commercial shipping is not wise for fragile telescopes, and then the telescope will have to come all the way back to the Hole in the Wall. I'm not looking forward to the process, but the chance that a telescope of this type might work on the float is too enticing. When John says something is broke, it's broke.

The telescope goes home with me – first via boat to Shinglemill, then via car to the airport, then via two airline connections to California, then to my house via taxi, then via FedEx to the factory. And then the whole process begins over again (in reverse).

On my next visit to the cabin, I have the telescope unpacked and on the deck the first clear afternoon, awaiting nightfall. When it is sufficiently dark, I go through the brief alignment process, dial up M57 in the telescope's database, wait for the purr of the gears, and there in the center of the eyepiece is the distinctive smoke-halo of the Ring Nebula. I am almost fearful of hitting the Go-To button again, but I do, and M13 (a globular cluster in Hercules) rotates into the center of the low-powered eyepiece. I change to a shorter focal length (higher power) eyepiece and easily resolve stars in the outer edge of the cluster. Success!

M13, globular cluster in the constellation of Hercules

Even after several hours of celestial observation on the float, the Go-To function still takes me (almost flawlessly) to each newly selected object. Sometimes, the float moves slightly during that period, but even then I can usually avoid a complete realignment by using the simple resynchronization process for new objects, and everything returns to normal.

There is a lot I can do to promote accurate alignment and tracking of the telescope. I walk very softly with minimal movements on the deck, avoid nights with any wind (a waste of time, considering the float's movement), and try to get my observing done without delay while the deck moves slowly to a new position. Having all my star charts, eyepieces, filters, and other observing equipment at-hand on the deck prevents excessive walking back-and-forth, which upsets the float. That's an improved observing technique that reduces the float movement and simultaneously increases my viewing efficiency.

After the hassle of shipping the telescope back for repairs, the accuracy of the alignment system becomes a joy. When an occasional night boat moves through the channel, the float will rock, and I'll watch a deep-sky object bob up and down in the eyepiece. When the rocking stops, the object usually returns to the center of the field of view, or close enough to center with a quick resynchronization.

The float moves, but then returns to its exact-same starting point. I never would have guessed that a floating cabin would be a stable mount for a precision telescope.

If I sound like an astronomical fanatic, that's because I am. My fanaticism has come and gone (and now come again) throughout my lifetime. I ask you to relate something in your own life to my passion for astronomy. Maybe you will be enlightened, as I have been, regarding how a temporarily discarded dream is able to actualize itself to the ultimate level. All that's needed is the right opportunity. In my case, the opportunity is a floating cabin in Canada, an unlikely source of astronomical inspiration.

My enthusiasm regarding astronomy was demonstrated at an early age, culminating in the purchase of a large astronomical telescope. At least it was large for a 14-year-old boy. A 4-inch refractor was the culmination of a lot of saved nickels and dimes from my newspaper route, but once I possessed the telescope, it became an immediate logistics problem. One of the reasons that so many enthusiastic amateur astronomers lose interest in their passion so quickly is because of the weight and bulkiness of large telescopes. Most of the older models have huge counterweights for the equatorial mount. Computer-driven models no longer require equatorial alignment, so weight and structural simplicity (and price) are the immediate benefits.

My original 4-inch scope was heavy and difficult to move from the house to the yard. Plus, where would Mom allow her son to store this monstrosity? The solution was an observatory, since all real astronomers have observatories. Now I just had to convince Dad to fund it and build it. He reacted more favorably than I would have guessed, but I noticed that it didn't look at all like an observatory. In fact, it was a shed that was constructed at the rear of the garage, with a regular-size door that made it a special chore to deploy the telescope and its bulky tripod to its observing position in the yard. But the shed was adjacent to our backyard where the streetlights interfered minimally with a young astronomer's night sessions. It was dark enough here that Dad was moderately injured when he tripped over a low garden fence while trying to simultaneously walk and observe the first Sputnik satellite.

The question might be asked: Why not simply use the garage for telescope storage, since it has a bigger door? One answer is that the shed gave me a place to call my own, with a display area for posters and a storage area for books – an observatory. I noted that the observatory converted quickly to a tool shed as soon as I left for college, which undoubtedly explained my father's enthusiasm for the project.

Have you identified a passion of your own that equates to my zeal for astronomy? Maybe it's a sport or a field of study that you've always dabbled in but never pursued seriously. That's what happened to me; astronomy turned out to be something that seemed, at the time, a dead end. I headed toward a career in astronomy, only to realize that astronomers don't do what I love – observational work at the eyepiece. And the job market for astronomers isn't exactly a booming enterprise.

My University of Buffalo physics degree incorporated only two astronomy courses – an introductory class that was so basic that it was intended for non-physics majors and a celestial mechanics course so difficult that I barely passed. The celestial mechanics class was primarily advanced differential calculus, not exactly what I had expected when I watched the dance of Jupiter's moons.

During a brief post-college summer stint as an astronomer's assistant at the U.S. Naval Observatory in Washington, DC, I plowed into the sudden realization that professional astronomy was not where I wanted to go. I spent most of that summer sitting in front of a "blinker," a photographic plate viewer that allows astronomers to compare two photos of the same star field to detect variations in stellar brightness or position. This wasn't what I signed up for in Astronomy 101. In fact, most of the astronomy jobs at the Naval Observatory were office-oriented. Looking through telescopes was not part of the deal.

I also noticed that all of the real astronomers around me were extremely intelligent and exceedingly specialized. The competition was intense, while I just wanted to kick around looking at marvelous objects through a telescope. There was no way I could keep up with a real astronomer's attention to math and specialized computational details. It was quite a letdown, but it was also a turning point in my life that allowed me to develop in new directions, such as aviation. I didn't totally turn my back on astronomy, but I stopped looking through telescopic eyepieces for nearly 20 years.

If you're like me and have an ingrained passion for something like astronomy, it never really goes away. For me, it was an infatuation that simply went into hibernation. Living in city-folk places in California with names like Burbank and Pomona didn't promote my interest in observational astronomy. There are a lot of great dark-sky observing sights in the deserts of southern California, but in the era of bulky tripods, large reflector telescope design, and equatorial counterweights, hauling equipment to the observing site was not a pleasant prospect. One of the current officers of my California astronomy club has a 12-inch reflector (a giant piece of equipment for an amateur), and he keeps it permanently stored in his van for semi-portable use. It's a pretty full van. Now there's a real astronomical fanatic!

During my hibernation from observational astronomy, I still read everything I could get my hands on that had to do with the sky, attended all of the Astronomical Society of the Pacific conferences, and dreamed of someday operating an advanced astronomical telescope at a future home in some dark location. But I wasn't there yet and had no idea where that dark site would be.

The advent of compact computer-controlled Go-To instruments and a floating cabin in Canada changed all of that overnight. I wasn't looking for it, but it found me. Maybe that's the way the best wonders of life pop up on our doorstep. Maybe that's also the reason that life takes so many unexpected excursions from where we point ourselves.

\* \* \* \* \*

The cliff next to our cabin is so tall that Polaris, the North Star, dips in and out of the treetops as the cabin gyrates through its minor movements. Since Polaris' elevation above the cabin is 52 degrees (its elevation equates to latitude), that implies the north side of my sky is mostly covered by granite. To the east, Goat is a huge wall that ascends from the water, blocking the rising stars. All astronomical objects climb out of the top (or side) of Goat at their assigned place in the granite, each at their expected season and time. To the west is the mountain wall of Chippewa Bay (not quite as dominating as Goat), and that leaves the south. The earth's celestial equator is tipped equal to the earth's inclination, so you can't see very far south of the celestial equator at this northerly location. Not only are few southern hemisphere constellations visible (you can see over half of them from most locations in the United States), even the northern hemisphere's constellations are severely limited by the physical walls of the Hole.

At Canadian latitudes you get to see a lot of circumpolar constellations (they move around Polaris without setting), but I have a cliff wall to the north. In other words, as an amateur astronomer, I have to be pretty efficient with my observing window, because it isn't very large. But give me a little window, and I'll give you a big view. The darkness, transparency, seeing, and lack of light pollution make all the difference in the world. And my telescope never sits more than a few feet from the dark sky.

The 5-inch Maksutov-Cassegrain (lens in front, mirror in back) is so compact that it fits in the kitchen. When you live on a float, everything has its place or you run out of places, so the telescope tripod is placed strategically so the floor surface is still usable for boot storage, and the adjacent kitchen table is at least half serviceable for food-like functions.

The telescope easily slips out through the patio door onto the deck and is then positioned near the edge of the deck over a 2-foot-diameter wooden spool that originally stored steel cabin restraint cables (these spools make great tables and decorative cabin fixtures). This is a location promoting maximum sky coverage. The cable spool provides an excellent table for eyepieces and charts, right under the tripod. Movement around the tripod and spool is a bit tricky. One false step and you're in the water in the middle of the night, but you learn to improve your sure-footedness when you live on a float. The only light pollution is your own, so darkness is your friend.

The best observing is during the winter at this latitude, particularly if you like the freezing cold. The nights in December and January are over 15 hours long (not including twilight), so there's a lot to see, and you can begin in total darkness shortly after 5 PM. Dew is often a problem on cold winter nights on the float, and even with my telescope's dew cap (a plastic extension over the lens), four hours is usually the maximum observing time before dew on the primary lens terminates the observing session. Once dew forms on the front lens, there is no solution other than to warm the telescope inside. I've found that 4-hour winter sessions are all that my California body can stand anyway, so sometimes it's fun to awaken in the middle of the night (or even 5 AM) and begin the observing session. You still have a lot of time before dawn.

Winter viewing, for me, includes the Canadian layered-look, with a one-piece snowsuit as the final cover. A head-and-ears mask is particularly appreciated, as are several layers of gloves, making movement of telescope controls, eyepiece focusing, and computer settings even more challenging.

Viewing in the summer is ergonomically superior. Long pants and shirts are still recommended because of possible mosquito attacks (even gloves and hat, just in case). But the nights are very short (a little over three hours of total darkness in June and July), with the sun dipping below the horizon in the far northwest and rising in the nearby northeast. The sun is never very far below the horizon, but the cliff to the north extends far enough (assisted by Goat) so that twilight is somewhat muted.

Summer is a season requiring maximum efficiency in the observing schedule. I keep a list of prime objects ready to go, and then often find myself falling asleep before midnight, when the darkness finally arrives. If you miss the midnight start, the only solution is to awaken before 3 AM. Otherwise, you've lost the entire short summer night.

✶ ✶ ✶ ✶ ✶

**I**'ve developed celestial friendships – objects that I go back to again and again. One of my goals is to view all 110 of the Messier deep-sky objects, but my progress is slowed when I return to my favorites hundreds of times instead. The galaxies M81 and M82 are visible in the same field of view of a low-power eyepiece, and M82 is one of my favorites. It's limited to spring and the early nighttime hours during summer, when the Big Dipper rides above the granite cliff to the north. M82 is an irregular galaxy shaped like a cigar. In my imagination, it looks like a spaceship. In the telescope, a jagged rift of darkness rips across the center of the galaxy. The rift forms the windows of the spacecraft.

Spiral Galaxy M81 (left) and irregular galaxy M82 in Ursa Major

M82 handles higher magnifications well, but I also enjoy studying it in the low-power eyepiece, where it sits next to its sister galaxy, M81. Astronomers think M81 plowed through (or near) M82 recently (in astronomical terms), triggering new star formation in its gravitational wake. I can easily visualize this time-lapse movement as I stare at the two galaxies. Visualization and imagination are key ingredients that make astronomy intoxicating for me. I can return to M82 night-after-night, see the same rifts, and imagine new things each time. Tonight, I imagine the aliens in the passing cigar-shaped spaceship waving to me as they speed past.

Other astronomical friends rise over Goat at their appointed time in their expected locations. Their familiarity and predictability are reassuring. The Pleiades pop out of a specific ragged rock area on top of Goat at about 7 PM in late December (the precise time can be calculated based on the specific date). My celestial friends rise over Goat four minutes earlier each night, marking the slow march of the seasons.

In winter, I await Orion at 8 PM in late December, for it contains M42, the luminous Orion Nebula. The constellation, lying on its side, initially protrudes from the edge of Goat, seemingly pushed out from within the mountain's south wall. With a narrowband filter threaded onto my medium-power eyepiece, M42 shines like a cosmic neon sign, presenting the Orion stellar nursery. If I live long enough, maybe I'll see a new star born here. Embedded in the nebula is the Trapezium, easily resolved into its individual trapezoid of stars, and a good test of the night's seeing conditions.

> "You know Orion always comes up sideways.
> Throwing a leg over our fence of mountains,
> And rising on his hands, he looks in on me
> Busy outdoors by lantern-light with something
> I should have done by daylight..."
>
> **Robert Frost**
> **from *The Star Splitter* (1923)**

When the planets are visible through my constricted granite window frame, I make repeated visits to these objects, bright in comparison to the challenge of deep-sky wonders. Jupiter's moons change their position so rapidly that significant movement can be detected over the course of a night's observing session. Transits of the moons across the surface of the planet are always exciting, the shadow of the satellite forming a tiny dot that moves across the entire surface of Jupiter in a few hours.

The cloud bands of Jupiter are intricate or subdued, depending upon the seeing conditions at the moment of observation. A slight change in atmospheric stability can make a significant difference in planetary detail. I breathe slowly, relax my viewing eye, and use averted vision to tune my vision to the details of the dark. I wait for those few seconds when the earth's atmosphere suddenly stabilizes and reveals planetary details. It is an opportunity that comes and goes quickly. I switch to a high-power eyepiece, pushing the magnification to 297 power. This is the practical limit for the telescope, and only perfect seeing conditions can handle it.

Saturn is another test of the night's atmospheric conditions. The Cassini Division in the rings is the best test, with finer divisions more the product of imagination (in this small telescope) than reality. There's little to see in Saturn's cloud bands, but the ever-splendid rings make the planet impossible to pass up on any night that it fits into my granite-bordered window.

Small critters move around the deck in the dark. They aren't a problem (well, there was the pack rat that sat on my lounge chair and pooped on the cushion every night), but they do get your attention when you're in the middle of an intense session at the eyepiece. In general, mice enjoy float life (and the food goodies inside the cabin), so a series of mouse invasions while we are away lead to a new procedure – remove the gangplank to shore. Problem solved.

Sometimes, just as I'm settling in with a deep-sky Messier object that requires visual and mental concentration along with simultaneous eye relaxation and the use of averted version, a mouse or squirrel zips below me on one of the brow logs. They do this just to frighten me. (Is that the USO?) It works – I shine my flashlight, with red lens to enhance my night vision, down between the deck boards, which are fully open to the float structure and water below. In my imagination, I see a leg of the giant USO, although the next day it seems more like a mouse. In reality, I seldom see a critter on the float at night. And the good news is that even with only a fleeting glimpse, these creatures look too small to be the USO.

M42, emission nebula in Orion, with Trapezium at bottom

# Chapter 15

# NDB-DME Approach

O nce you leave the border cities behind, Piper Arrows aren't a common airplane. Most small Canadian aircraft are on floats, and those that aren't have a robust bush flying appearance. An Arrow is definitely a city-folk design.

Several years ago, flying into Dawson City in the Yukon, an air traffic controller began pointing out traffic a long way out. When there is so little traffic on the airways, the controllers tend to give you more information than you sometimes need.

"Arrow 997, you have traffic at 30 miles, climbing out of Dawson City, a DC-3. He'll be headed southbound on the airway as closing traffic at niner thousand."

"997 will be looking for the traffic," I reply.

This is a nice gesture by air traffic control, but seeing another aircraft at 30 miles is impossible. Yet a DC-3 is an exciting airplane, so I'll be looking for this classic.

A few minutes later, there is another radio call.

"Yukon Air Two-Three, you have traffic at 12 o'clock, 25 miles, opposite direction, a Pace Arrow at eight thousand."

"Roger, we'll be looking for the Pace Arrow," replies the DC-3.

A series of updates are received for the next five minutes, as we continue to close with the DC-3, and the controller keeps referring to us as a Pace Arrow. It is no big deal, and I don't feel it is necessary to correct him.

After awhile, Margy asks: "What's a Pace Arrow?"

I'm not an expert at aircraft identification, especially older aircraft, so I tell her that I think it is an older single-engine airplane that looks a bit like a Piper Tri-Pacer. Pace Arrows are probably a lot more common here than Piper Arrows. The DC-3 pilot acts comfortable with the identification instructions.

The controller continues to keep the DC-3 pilot and us appraised of each other's position, although we remain far out of visual range and are not a collision hazard, especially with a 1000-foot altitude separation. Finally, we are close enough to see each other.

"Yuke Two-Three, the Pace Arrow is now at your 12 o'clock position – two miles, at eight thousand."

"We have the Pace Arrow in sight," replies the DC-3 pilot.

"Roger. Maintain visual separation from the Pace Arrow," instructs the controller.

A few seconds later, we see the DC-3, her old fat wings lumbering above us on the airway. It is a memorable sight. DC-3s and Pace Arrows are the kind of classic aircraft plying the airways of Canada, not Piper Arrows.

Later that evening, we are on a small riverboat, headed for a touristy (but tasty) salmon dinner at a well-advertised restaurant upstream. Dawson City is a major transition point between the Canadian Yukon and Alaska, with a small barge-like ferry shuttling vehicles across the river. Our riverboat driver slows to allow the ferry to exit the dock, and we peer at the vehicles nestled on the ferry deck. The one nearest to us is a huge RV with the factory brand in large black letters: "Pace Arrow." Canadian air traffic controllers don't see a lot of Piper Arrows, but they must see some Pace Arrows. Maybe the DC-3 pilot was looking for an RV with wings.

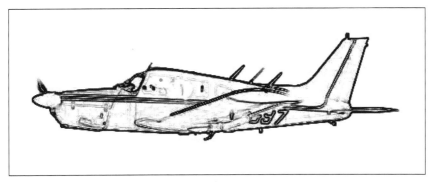

\* \* \* \* \*

One of the biggest differences between flying in the U.S. and Canada is the increased utilization of non-directional beacons in Canada. NDBs are seldom used in the U.S., and that is fine with American pilots. They are tricky to use for navigation, requiring a bit of mental math, and they don't always lead to an accurate instrument landing. These beacons are subject to static interference and fit appropriately into their assigned category – "non-precision" approaches. Pilots are tested on NDB procedures on the U.S. instrument flight test, and then seldom use these fickle navaids again.

So when you cross the Canadian border and encounter NDB airways and instrument approaches, it's a bit disconcerting. I used to tell fellow pilots that there are two things I avoid: thunderstorms and NDB approaches. Now I have no choice but to use NDBs, or I won't get to many Canadian destinations.

Powell River Airport has one of these infamous NDB approaches, but it is enhanced by distance measuring equipment (DME) at the NDB site. That's a big improvement, since DME provides range information. On this approach, I still don't know quite where I am in terms of direction from the airport (using the NDB), but I do know exactly how far away I am (using the DME). It's like having a gauge in your car that tells you exactly how many miles you are from a store you're trying to find, without any knowledge of what street it is on or what direction to drive.

Pacific Coastal Airlines, unlike American amateurs, executes the NDB-DME approach into Powell River regularly and flawlessly. Of course, I don't know what obscenities are being expressed in their cockpits, but I do watch them fly this approach like clockwork in all kinds of ugly weather. I suspect that they are carefully backing themselves up with satellite navigation equipment.

Pacific Coastal aircraft are small by airline standards (turboprops rather than jets), and they point these airplanes into some of the most vicious weather on earth. If you don't believe that, you should stand on the balcony of my condo, overlooking the chuck, on a dreary winter night with rain pouring down and southeast winds roaring up the Malaspina Strait. I'm often in my condo when these exact conditions occur, since going up the lake on nights like this is not on the recommended list.

At the appointed time, I hear the drone of turboprops nearly overhead, as another Pacific Coastal flight starts outbound from the NDB (located on the airport). The prescribed route on the NDB-DME approach takes these aircraft straight past my condo toward Harwood Island, and on nights like this they are usually in the clouds when they start outbound. The growl of the twin turboprops fades in the distance and nearly disappears as the invisible aircraft makes its procedure turn, a complete course reversal. Now the airplane hurls back inbound, following the nebulous NDB signal, while simultaneously descending and looking for the runway lights in the rain. The DME is counting down in the cockpit now, and (with luck) the aircraft breaks out of the clouds in a mighty roar right over my balcony. As good as these pilots are, I'm sure the pucker factor is pretty high at this point on the approach.

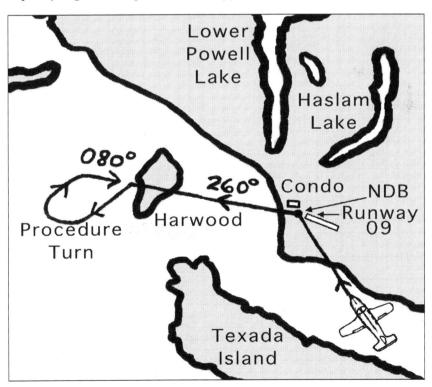

I fly the Pacific Coastal route between Powell River and Vancouver as a passenger several times each year. Usually those flights
are in the bad-weather months, since summer is my Piper Arrow's
time in the sun. Planning a trip on a specific schedule from California to Powell River in the winter would be impossible in an Arrow, regardless of flight experience. Aleutian lows wind up tight and
toss their isobars across the Strait of Georgia in the winter, with
winds beyond the limits of small aircraft. On the other hand, Pacific
Coastal aircraft are not much larger or more elaborately equipped
than my Arrow, so I particularly admire the job these pilots accom-
plish day after day.

Often it is a familiar Pacific Coastal pilot and copilot on the Vancouver route, and I feel that I know them. I notice how they gently
(or not so gently) reduce the throttles at the beginning of the descent
on the NDB-DME approach. I wish that I could be listening on their
intercom to determine how they really feel about this instrument
arrival, particularly as they begin the procedure turn over Harwood
Island. And what does it look like from the cockpit the moment they
break out of the clouds and see my balcony?

Once, when flying in my Arrow with John, we landed at Bella
Coola when the weather wasn't looking very good. The overcast layer was lowering rapidly as we refueled. Quite a bit of time elapsed

before we were ready to depart (we simply had to go fishing in the river next to the airport), and I was glad to see a Pacific Coastal aircraft arrive. It's always nice to ask another pilot what is really out there before you depart. An overcast layer looks a lot different from below than from on-top.

Pacific Coastal doesn't waste any time, so they parked and unloaded quickly. By the time I reached the airport office, the pilots were kicked back with their feet on the table, reading the local newspaper. I recognized the female pilot immediately, since I had ridden on her aircraft several times on the route between Powell River and Vancouver. I approached her like an old friend, since she introduced herself to me each time she gave the Vancouver passenger briefing.

"Jill, what weather did you find in Burke Channel on the way in?" I asked.

She gave me a strange stare – Do I know you? Then she lowered her feet from the table and recited the conditions that she had encountered on the approach to Bella Coola. Once she understood that I was departing the airport, she gave me lots of pertinent data about weather conditions all the way to Port Hardy, and that made me feel very comfortable with the situation. As I left the office, I glanced back and saw her inspect me to determine just where we had met. Then she kicked her feet up on the table again and continued reading her newspaper.

\* \* \* \* \*

**I** decide to join the Westview Flying Club for a variety of reasons. I need a storage location for my old Ford and boat trailer while I am away, and a hangar is ideal for that purpose. The Flying Club rents hangars, and mine will serve a dual purpose for alternating storage of my airplane and car.

When flying into the airport, a car is needed, and what better location for my vehicle than right on the airport under protective cover? Security is good at airports, so that is a bonus for things stored in the hangar. And once the car is removed, the hangar serves as a home for my airplane.

I rent the hangar in the spring, with my Arrow still in California. I depart Powell River, leaving my old car in the hangar. Upon return with the Arrow that summer, I park in front of the hangar, remove the car, and begin to push the Arrow back into her new home. It doesn't fit.

Actually, all looks okay at first, since the wings clear the hangar walls fine. But the tail slot is too small by only a few inches. No one owns an Arrow at this airport, and Arrow tails are slightly wider than other aircraft of this category. It is time for a different hangar.

In the process, I receive a nice upgrade. The new hangar is in the first row, facing the runway. My Arrow loves to watch other airplanes when she is idle, and this structure is more carport than hangar. The front is wide open, and my Arrow sits out of the weather, watching Canadian airplanes takeoff and land. She loves it!

The arrangement is perfect – until the RVs arrive. As a Flying Club member, I am expected to participate in other membership activities besides simply using the hangar, and I desire to be involved. This will be a good way to learn about Canadian aviation, and I want the club to prosper. One method of prospering involves renting vacant hangars to RV owners who need a storage area. What an ideal way to make some money for the club – double-book my hangar with RVs when my airplane is in California (push the car and boat trailer to the side), and then move the RVs out when the Arrow returns.

This is a fine plan, except pretty soon the RVs take over my hangar to the extent that it is impossible to move the car (precariously wedged between a boat trailer and a motor home) when I arrive. Or I land in the Arrow, taxi to the hangar, and find the interior full of RVs. It becomes a bit of a challenge, but I support the inconveniences of the situation for two reasons. First, I'm not in town that often. And second, John has to deal with it.

John takes his responsibilities regarding my equipment seriously. While I am in California, he maintains and keeps track of my stuff with dedication. And prior to my return, he starts everything up to make sure it is in proper operational order (winter can take a toll) and prepares everything for my arrival. He takes pride in maintaining my equipment with care, and finding the hangar full of RVs just when I am due to arrive is discouraging for him. Worse yet, finding someone to move the RVs is always a challenge. At the same time, he has to listen to my supporting arguments for the double-booking.

John becomes a common visitor at the airport as he tries to work out the game of hangar musical chairs. Over time, he becomes more recognized as a member of the Flying Club than I.

* * * * *

Flying with John is an enlightening experience. Each time we fly together, I'm impressed with his ability to distinguish discrete landmarks from the air. Of course, he knows the region intimately from the ground, but things look a lot different from the cockpit. Although the scope of the aerial view helps orient your sense of location, those who fly only occasionally have a difficult time putting things in perspective. Not John – he knows where he is and where everything else is from his position in the air, and that even applies to regions beyond his normal ground range. On our flights to Vancouver, he quickly identifies landmarks in Howe Sound, a place he has never been.

One day, on a flight from Bella Coola to Bella Bella, far from anyplace John has ever been, he states matter-of-factly soon after reaching cruise altitude: "Hey, look – there's Ocean Falls." This tiny community, wedged in the remote fjord of Cousins Inlet, must be stared at directly and from just the right angle to be seen from the air. He does this entirely without a map, and he is absolutely certain that it is the remote community. I check my aeronautical chart closely – it is indeed Ocean Falls.

* * * * *

Returning from Vancouver, I cancel my instrument flight clearance near Sechelt, and John and I turn north to inspect an area west of Mount Alfred where John and his quad buddies are considering blazing a trail. The area is vaguely familiar to me from the air, but the numerous mountains, inlets, and lakes provide a blend of geography that makes everything look similar. Aided by my GPS moving-map, there is no doubt where we are, but the geography is complex, and I repeatedly recheck my aerial position in this high-country.

We continue up Jervis Inlet, identify the buildings at Malibu Rapids and gaze into Princess Louisa Inlet to our right. Then we bank to the left, south of Mount Alfred, and scan the area that John is considering for trail development. John looks ahead and identifies the lakes to the west.

"There's Emma Lake," says John. I have no doubt that he is correct. "Do you see the cabin with the red roof?" he asks.

I barely see the blue dot that is Emma Lake. John directs my attention to the south side of the lake as we approach closer. Sure enough, there is the red roof.

"Got it!" I say. "I see the red roof."

"I've been there," says John. "That's a skookum cabin."

As we begin our descent south of Beartooth, John provides an on-going verbal tour of the mountainous region. It makes sense on my GPS moving map, but John has it all in his brain. It is not just a two-dimensional chart that he sees. It is a 3-D map in his mind.

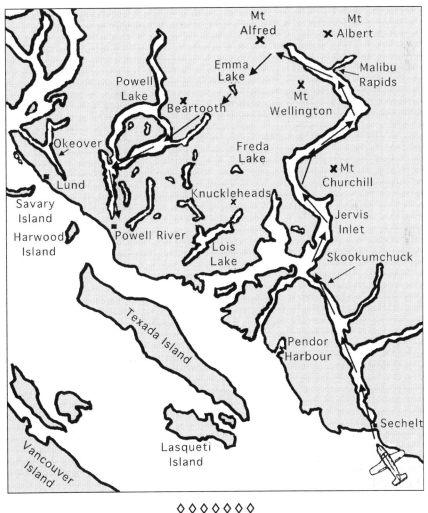

◊ ◊ ◊ ◊ ◊ ◊ ◊

# Chapter 16

## Intersection in the Wilderness

The basic dropped-object rule of the float is quickly learned – don't pull anything out of your pocket on the deck that you don't want lost in the water. Besides the 360 degrees of surrounding water, the deck itself consists of open planking. Deck boards are generally six inches wide, but a good float construction engineer (John) uses whatever lumber is available. It all blends in beautifully, but there are gaps between the boards that range from an eighth of an inch to a full half-inch. Rain runs off smoothly through these cracks, but it's amazing what else fits through such openings when dropped at an unlucky angle.

On my first day of float cabin ownership, I am busy checking out the shed. John's message, through the barrister who closes the deal for us, is that he has removed his valuables from the shed, and all else is ours. The shed is locked, so the contents remain a mystery. The curtainless window doesn't help a bit, since it is perched 10 feet above the water. I am intrigued by what might be found in the shed, and the barrister provides me with the padlock key for the shed's mysteries.

The door creaks open, and I step into the void. As my eyes adjust to the darkness, a critter (probably a mouse) scampers across the floor, and I jump as if it is a bear. For this first visit, I decide to view the contents from the safety of the shed's entry area – no more scary mice, please!

In the shed are a variety of unexplained treasures, including some freshly cut lumber, segments of rain gutter, an old-style VHF boat radio, various lengths and diameters of rope, several cans of paint, unmarked cans of liquids (several on a wooden shelf that surround the interior at eye level), and a blue baseball cap with a large "W" logo. None of these items seem immediately valuable, but I treasure them for their unspoken history. Most of these treasures remain in the shed to this day. The blue cap has a position of prominence on its original hook.

I take a new combination padlock out of my pocket. I have decided that keyed padlocks are going to be a problem, since the number of locks is already multiplying. I close the shed door and replace the keyed padlock with the combination lock. I grasp the old padlock and key, and step onto the bridge to the float.

Within two steps, the key falls gracefully from my hand into the water. Although I am only a few feet from shore, the key is doomed to a watery grave the moment it falls. I watch it drop toward the depths in sunken-leaf motion, with short frequency fluttering back-and-forth. The water is so clear that I am able to follow the key until it disappears at an estimated depth of 20 feet, and that is the mere beginning of its journey to the bottom. I immediately realize this would be a ruined day, if I had not replaced the keyed-lock with a combo model. If you don't want something lost in the water, keep it in your pocket until you are inside the cabin or firmly in your boat.

On the second day of float cabin ownership, I am pounding nails on the transition float. The deck boards have a few protruding nail heads that really don't need attention, but I am already getting into the groove of keeping my float in prime condition. At home in California, you'll never find a hammer in my hand.

On the second board in sequence, the hammer comes down at an awkward angle, jarring my wrist. I let go of the hammer, and it arcs perfectly toward the awaiting water and disappears in a splash.

I go back into the cabin, criticizing myself for my carelessness. I remove a small hammer from my tool kit. It's a substandard tool, but it will be big enough to finish the job. This time, I wisely loop a knot around the neck of the hammer with a 3-foot piece of thin rope. I tie the rope around my wrist and finish the nail-pounding job. Well, I almost finish the job. While pounding the nails in the final row of boards, the hammer swings awkwardly out of my hand, reaches the full extension of the rope, and slips flawlessly out of the noose that is loosely tied. Kerplunk – another precise water shot and another hammer to a watery grave. This is day number two, with a key and two hammers already in the drink.

* * * * *

One day, as I depart the cabin for a two-day cruise on the chuck, I swap my propane tanks. It's an easy process, since the propane storage area is equipped with two tanks so that one is always standing ready when you run out of fuel. The current tank is not yet completely empty, but I am concerned with running out of propane while I am gone, since I'll be leaving the propane refrigerator operating. I move the nearly empty tank to the back deck where it won't be seen by boaters passing by. Normally, I would take the propane tank to town for refill, but it's an involved process – load the tank into the boat, offload it from the boat and roll it along the dock to the car, and then via car to the local propane station. Subsequently, all is repeated in reverse, except with a heavier tank on the return trip. This tank can wait for another day. When I return two days later, the tank is gone.

As I contemplate a story for John that will justify my stupidity, I realize that nothing will suffice. The tank wasn't stolen – it was blown off the deck in my absence and floated to who-knows-where.

I hunt around the Hole, hoping to find the tank against the shore or jammed against the float of a neighboring cabin. No luck – I will need to explain what happened to John. The tank is long gone.

I decide it is best to face the music by simply explaining my fool-hardiness. (You can't explain your stupidity, but you can explain that you are stupid.) As I tell John about the loss, he looks particularly concerned. Why is he so grim? This isn't a crime – it is merely bad judgment on my part. John doesn't say anything. He merely shakes his head in disgust.

When I am finished with my lame story, John explains that he found a propane tank floating in the middle of the Hole and celebrated the find. As a true beachcomber, this was the floating discovery of the year for him, and now he has to give it back. I can tell he considered (briefly) simply acknowledging my stupidity and sending me out to buy another tank in order to teach me a lesson.

✳ ✳ ✳ ✳ ✳

I'm constantly looking for ways to challenge John's creative mind. You might consider this continual process as attempts to trick him.

One evening I am playing with my model Coast Guard cutter, experimenting with its range and maneuverability. I guide the re-mote-control vessel into the rear area of the breakwater and ponder how to get the model boat into the natural swimming pool. How would John tackle such a challenge? The route is clearly blocked by a log, tethered at both ends. The prevailing breeze is from the south, pushing the log tightly into the pool.

I devise a plan to slip the model boat into the corner of the pool where the log rests against the float. I will push the log outward from the pool, using the model cutter's tiny twin engines, and then slip the boat over the submerged tether. I'll carefully coast over the rope with the props turned off. It is a good plan, but it takes me three tries and nearly a half-hour to get the model boat into the swim-ming pool. Each time I fail, I reposition the remote-control boat to attempt another entry. This will be a challenge for John.

The next day at Number 3, I tell John I have prepared a demanding contest for him, and I announce that I completed the challenge the night before, admitting it took three tries. I give him a few details of the puzzle, explaining that he must first circle the cabin clockwise with the cutter, under my instructions. I add some extra obstacles along the way to distract him from the final swimming pool entry, and off he goes.

John backs the boat out of its miniature dock, around Rubber Ducky #1 and out and around several designated stumps. He follows my instructions, directing the model cutter under the bridge (deftly angling the boat under two dangling float cables), and then reverses course and guides the boat out through the main breakwater entrance and along the outside of the breakwater logs. As the boat heads west, I provide blow-by-blow commentator coverage for this "International Sports Challenge":

"Captain John's grip on the remote-control lever is firm – he is obviously a determined competition boater," I say into an imaginary microphone. "He's trying to beat the national champion in this event and the established world record."

Ten-year-old twin girls from the adjacent cabin are just coming out of the far end of the Hole in their matching yellow plastic kayaks, and they face the model boat head-on as it passes between them and the log breakwater. The twins giggle at the sight of the model cutter but keep on paddling. To the model boat, the small kayaks are on the scale of the *Queen Mary*, and John now faces swells that nearly swamp the tiny cutter. I speak into my imaginary microphone:

"And folks, the International Sports Challenge has detected sudden interference from two passing oceanliners in a reverse speed bump effect. But Captain John is keeping his ship pointed into these huge waves."

Finally, John approaches the log blocking the swimming pool. The south wind has firmly closed the entry.

"The trick is to get in," I say proudly.

"This is a good one," says John.

"I made it into the pool last night, but it wasn't easy," I remind him.

I can see his brain clicking as he stops the model boat about 10 feet from the log, his mind pondering the geometry. He starts forward again with the cutter, powering toward the end of the log that I successfully used as an entrance the evening before. After traveling a few feet, he cuts power and reverses the cutter's twin engines. He swings the boat around and begins backing it against the edge of the log, nudging the barrier farther closed with the rear of the cutter, the twin-props barely clearing the edge of the log. Then he quickly shifts into forward thrust and roars toward the far end of the pool. By the time he arrives at the other end, the log has rebounded fully open, and in the boat slips into the swimming area.

It's hard to fool John. Just when you think you've got him, he pulls an end-around reverse.

* * * * *

**F**riends and friends-of-friends sometimes show up on my float unannounced. One day, John is having lunch with me when a boat appears off my breakwater. Some of John's friends have heard he will be visiting me today, and they simply show up for a visit. The visit, in this case, lasts most of the afternoon.

Although I know only one of the five visitors, they all know John. As they offload their ice chest of beer, it looks like they have come to stay awhile, and they do.

Two of these new friends particularly enjoy the cliffside layout. They dive from the cliffs, higher than I really desire to watch, hitting the water with a harsh splash. After tiring of the diving, they don snorkels and diving masks (they came prepared for a day on my float), and I watch them snorkel along the breakwater and then along the side of the float. There are only a few places where they can reach the bottom during their dives, and one of these places is near the transition float.

After a lengthy time below the surface, one of the snorkelers comes up blowing water from his snorkel and victoriously holding a prized object high above his head. He spits the snorkel out of his mouth.

"Look at this rusty hammer!" he proudly announces.

"That could be a real relic," say John, the recognized expert on such topics. "It may have been down there for decades."

I simply keep my mouth shut.

* * * * *

**M**argy buys a truck, after a lot of shopping effort. For months, we watch the trucks that are for sale. Finally, the right one comes along, and John agrees that it meets his demanding specs. Now it is time for the first off-road test.

The morning begins for Margy and me with breakfast on the upper deck at the Shinglemill, a beautiful summer day with lots of activity at the boat launch ramp. It is a starkly bright morning, with the low sun reflecting sharply off the gentle ripples of water in the marina.

A yellow hardtop stern-drive is adeptly launched from its trailer and quickly tied to the dock for loading. As the trailer pulls away, a 20-foot canvas-top boat is backed into the shallow launch ramp water by a hefty dark-green pickup truck. Two healthy-looking women exit the truck, maybe sisters. One of the T-shirted women jumps onto the dock and positions both a bow and stern line from the boat in front of her on the dock. The other woman strides ankle-deep into the launch ramp water and then steps up onto the trailer's towbar to unhook the winch.

"Goin' up the lake, Heather?" yells a female voice from the fuel dock.

"Hey, Tara!" replies the woman poised on the trailer's towbar. "We haven't done this in years." They certainly look like they know what they are doing, regardless of this remark.

Winch unhooked, the woman reenters the truck, backs the trailered boat five feet farther into the water and abruptly applies the brakes. The canvassed-boat slides smoothly off the trailer into the awaiting rope-control of the woman on the dock. It's just like riding a bicycle – you never forget boat-launching skills.

From our lofty perch on the restaurant deck, we spot a boat we have never seen before, tucked into a remote corner beyond the fuel dock. A quad sits aboard, cross-wise on wooden supports mounted on the aft deck. Since it is a new and very unique boat (to us), I take a picture for John.

Leaving the Shinglemill, we drive three miles north of town to
Wilde Road, where John sometimes enters the network of forest service roads to off-load his quad. I know he has been riding the trail
to the Bunsters lately, so I hope we can surprise him by meeting at
the offload area. It's just about the right time of day.

Because I'm forever following John on remote trails, I have a
bad habit of not paying attention to the landmarks, relying on his
guidance instead. Today, we make the wrong turn on Wilde Road
and end up on an entry drive to an area of houses. There is an intersection ahead where Margy can make a three-point turnaround,
a good exercise for her truck driving skills.

But the turnaround does not go as planned. As Margy backs
the truck for the second "point," she misjudges the length of the
vehicle and the layout of the intersection. The rear tires slip into the
roadside ditch. There is no way we are getting out using two-wheel
drive.

The rear wheels spin and spin, so it is the ideal opportunity to
try the four-wheel lever for the first time. We're so new to the vehicle
that we think we should turn off the engine to engage the lever. It's
a bit of overkill, but it's the safe side of the situation. However, after
engaging the four-wheel lever, the engine won't start, so we sit awkwardly crosswise in the road with our rear wheels in the ditch.

Margy maneuvers the four-wheel lever back and forth, but
there's not even a click when the starter is engaged. We try rocking
back and forth in our seats; John has mentioned something about
rocking the truck if the four-wheel system ever fails to engage. Nothing.

Oh, wait – check the gearshift lever. Put it in "Park." We have
ignition. We also have a reminder of our novice truck driving skills.

The truck comes out of the ditch just like it is supposed to, and
we're pleased with the 4-by-4 option that John insisted we purchase.
He's right again, and we've barely left town.

When we arrive at the quad off-load spot, there are no vehicles.
So we continue up the dirt road about five miles, entering an area
where four-wheel drive is a necessity. Margy proceeds slowly and
cautiously but does a good job of controlling the vehicle in a non-

city environment with ruts and rocks big enough to keep our speed below 20 klicks. Some of the inclines are challenging to the point where my ol' Ford Tempo would be out of luck and dragging bottom. In our book, we're really truckin'.

We reach the turnoff to Chippewa Lake, a road we have been on with our quads, and we know it is far beyond our abilities in this truck. We easily maneuver to the shoulder of the wide intersection and stop where we are well clear for anyone coming up or down the mountain. It is time to trick John.

I take a picture of Margy and her new (to us) truck at this remote intersection. There are hundreds of intersections of dirt roads just like this throughout the area. It is a photo of an intersection in the middle of nowhere with trees and rocks along the side of a dirt road.

Later that evening, I print the two photos (the unidentified boat at the Shinglemill and Margy's truck at the intersection). Then I drive over to John's house to show him the photos. I fabricate an elaborate plan to introduce the photo of the intersection, but I haven't yet decided what clues to offer. There is no doubt John will be unable to identify this nondescript intersection of dirt roads at first glance, But I want to provide an increasingly detailed series of clues, beginning with some vague hints ("You've been at this intersection this week") and leading to more specific facts ("This is on the way to the Bunsters").

When I show John the first photo (the boat), he immediately identifies it. He drove by the lake today and saw the boat. (Remember, the boat was hidden from view, as far as I could tell, and it was just a drive-by for John rather than an inspection like we enjoyed from our high breakfast perch.) He also knows the guy who owns the boat and where he normally keeps it docked – at his cabin. I should have known that I couldn't surprise John with a photo of a boat.

Then I show him the photo of the road intersection with absolutely no comments except: "Take a look at this." I'll keep my hints in reserve for gradual release. I want to see how much information he requires to identify the location.

John looks at the photo for about three seconds, pauses reflec-
tively, and says: "That's the road to Chippewa Lake."

"No way!" I yell. He needs zero hints. I am utterly amazed.

"How could you possibly identify this intersection from hundreds
of others looking exactly the same?" I ask in awe.

"The small boulders along the side of the road are a give-away."
This is the only road with that specific alignment of rocks at the
intersection. It's hard to argue with that.

John's brain incorporates a photographic memory. He notices
absolutely everything and tucks it away to identify mystery photos
of road intersections in the middle of nowhere.

# Chapter 17

## Parking 28 ¢

Margy and I leave our float for town, not sure whether we are going riding or kayaking. So we have packed for both scenarios. My blue bag contains a set of long pants, mosquito repellent, and the rest of the common items needed for riding. My black bag includes suntan lotion and a waterproof container for the satellite phone. After breakfast, John will decide what we do today, as is often the case. Having lived a detailed day-to-day structure for decades, it is nice to have someone else flip the coin.

At John's house, the door is unlocked, so I walk in and hear the sound of the shower down the hallway. I pound on the bathroom door:

"Hurry up, I'm next!" I yell louder than necessary to be heard over the sound of the shower.

"No way, I just got in!" yells John. He knows I'm not here to take a shower.

Ten minutes later, upstairs, John pronounces his verdict:

"No riding for me today," he says. "We beat ourselves to death in Theodosia yesterday. Bro needs a day to recover. Me too, so I'll be going up the lake."

"Okay, Margy and I came prepared for riding or kayaking, so now we're gonna go kayaking. Any thoughts on Harwood versus Savary?"

"Well, the chuck looks calm, so either should work. But Lund is a bit of a zoo."

John is right. Summer in Lund is zooish, and it's the launching point for Savary Island. To get to Harwood Island, Gibson's Beach would be the launching point, and it is much less traveled.

"They are about the same paddling distance," I note. "We'd go nearly directly across to Harwood from Gibson's Beach, and the best route to Savary seems to be down the coast from Lund about a mile to the Iron Mine and then across."

"Either should be okay today," says John. The winds are light out of the northwest, so it will be an easy trip out and back.

We decide to avoid the zoo and start up Highway 101 for Gibson's Beach, but as I slow for the turn, an idea strikes me, and I accelerate past the turnoff.

"I just changed my mind," I tell Margy. "Hope you don't mind."

"No, Lund is fine with me."

"I just realized that I should drop some books at our retailers in Lund while we are this far north, and we might luck out on a parking spot. If we don't, we can always come back and launch from Gibson's."

"Sounds good to me," replies Margy. She's used to my constantly changing mind. If there was ever a woman who goes with the flow, it is Margy.

"We've never had much luck with parking in Lund, but maybe today is the day," I reply. I remember the busy launch ramp and the limited parking. It has never worked out well before, especially in the summer peak of tourists.

Lund seems farther away every trip. The 15-mile ride seems to take forever today, but finally we are past Dinner Rock and the end is near. As we wind down the final mile into Lund, there are cars parked on both sides of the road. The local newspaper has recently reported vandalism to vehicles parked here for extended periods. Lund residents aren't pleased with the popularity of Route 101 and its offshoot spurs as an overnight parking spot for visitors to Savary Island. They're mad as hell, and they ain't gonna take it anymore.

On the left is an ugly gravel pit, partly filled with water, and a huge sign: "Parking 28 ¢ a Day." The empty gravel pit passes quickly, but the big sign looms as a joke, or is it?

"Do you think they mean 28 dollars per day?" Margy asks. "28 cents isn't worth the effort."

"Maybe. Or it's just an expensive joke," I reply. "That's a really big sign." It would be a long walk to the hotel, but at least it's parking.

The mass of tourists greets us with a visual bang as we round the final corner to the hotel. Cars, trucks, and SUVs are parked everywhere. There is obviously no hope. Everything has changed since my visit the previous month – new buildings are to the left, adjacent to the newly reopened boardwalk. Lund is exploding, and it has nowhere to explode. The summer parking crisis is even worse than normal.

I pull behind the hotel. Straight ahead is an unexpected opportune parking spot, wide open and nearly adjacent to the north launch ramp. I go for it, beating a timid white van to the punch. My old Ford Tempo with the huge yellow banana on top wins a lot of psychological battles.

"Wait here while I deliver the books." It comes out like an order, but Margy understands the urgency. She'll guard the spot with her life. Already there are several cars pulling up close, hoping we are leaving rather than arriving.

By the time I return to the car, Margy has unloaded most of the kayak gear from the trunk, but she has a discouraging squint.

"No straps for the kayak carrier," she says. The two-wheel kayak carrier requires straps to hold the kayak. It will be a long haul to the launch ramp without the carrier. Our sea kayak is one of the heaviest.

"Those straps must be here," I say. "We used them last week at Gibson's Beach."

I pull everything out of the trunk, searching for the straps, and this trunk contains a lot of stuff. Then I pile all of the boxes, coats, and book promotional material back into the trunk. No straps. This is not a good start.

"We must have left them on the beach last week," I conclude.

"How about our roof carrier straps?" asks Margy.

Duh. The rooftop straps for the kayak connect to the wheeled-carrier better than the originals. In fact, if necessity is really the mother of invention, here's the perfect example. Life will be forever simpler with these ratchet-design straps.

But the launching process is far from complete. We still need to remove the kayak from the top of the car, and that's a challenge for a person as short as Margy. Once removed, the kayak is a tight fit between the Tempo and the truck parked next to us. Then we need to load all of the required paddling gear aboard the kayak – water bottles, satellite phone, two sets of paddles, cameras, bailing hand-pump, aft warning flagpole, and my inflatable backrest. Finally, we roll the kayak to the north launch ramp and down into the water.

Margy volunteers to take the wheeled-carrier back to the car, while I mind the kayak. Two dual kayaks, smaller than ours, are returning to the ramp with four giggly girls, one of whom is the guide. She has her hands full. The girl in her kayak is afraid to step out of the cockpit for fear of getting her feet wet. It's difficult to spend any time in a kayak without getting your feet wet.

Finally out of the water, the foursome (except the guide) begin complaining about having to carry the kayaks up the ramp. Maybe they expected a cruise ship trip rather than a kayak adventure.

As the whining girls are climbing the ramp, Margy arrives back at our kayak.

"Guess what we forgot?" she asks with a grim look.

"Whatever it is, we don't need it," I reply. I've been waiting (fairly patiently), and it's time to get going.

"Our life vests," she states pointedly.

"Oh," I acknowledge. There are few things that are absolutely required for a kayak journey, but life vests are a show-stopper.

Neither of us speaks for a few seconds, as our minds race to recover from this situation.

"How could we forget our life vests?" I stumble. Margy doesn't answer, since the answer is obvious. We've been juggling scenarios today, and our life vests sit in our boat at the Shinglemill, 15 miles away.

"Well, it was a good exercise in launching the kayak," I say with an amazing (to me) sense of acceptance. After all, there is nothing we can do about it, so I might as well relax. Wait a minute...

"Let's rent some life vests from Rockfish," I announce with a sense of unexpected solution. I remember the girls climbing the ramp in their ugly orange life vests. Why wouldn't Rockfish Kayak want to make some money off us by renting two of their life vests.

Margy volunteers to walk back up the ramp (again) to rent the vests while I continue to man the kayak. As I stand beside it, another idea comes to mind, so I leave the kayak partly beached and rush up the ramp to catch up with Margy. She is just exiting Rockfish with two puffy orange vests.

"How much?" I ask. Margy is surprised to see me here.

"Only four dollars each," she smiles back. That's amazing to me, but still...

"When does Rockfish close?" I ask.

"5 o'clock," is her response. I glance at my watch. It's already 2:30.

"Why not buy some new life vests?" I suggest. "I hate my old one, and I bet they have some nice ones for sale. There's no way we can go anywhere and be back by 5 o'clock."

"That's a bit of overkill, don't you think?" Margy is used to my quick (and sometimes stupid) decisions. But then she adds: "But they do have some nice vests in the shop." Obviously, the thought has passed through her mind as well.

We end up with two sporty (and expensive) yellow life vests. There is only one color and style on the rack, so we merely select our appropriate sizes and try them on. I hate it when Margy and I are dressed alike.

"Kind of a tough sell for you, wasn't it?" I say to the girl clerk as she rings up the total.

"I guess so," is her reply. She doesn't understand my sense of humor.

"Don't you think we'll look cute in matching vests?" I ask.

"You bet," she replies. She definitely doesn't understand my sense of humor.

But I love my new life vest. It is more comfortable than my old vest, and you can never have enough life vests. We prove that today.

Now we are <u>finally</u> ready to go, looking spiffy in our matching yellow attire. We paddle around the fuel dock and survey the new Lund. And it is new – Nancy's Bakery has been replaced by an ice-cream store, and Nancy's is in a new building by the boardwalk. The restaurant at the end of the boardwalk is open again, after a troubling period of inactivity. Even the wharfinger's office looks recently refurbished. There are people everywhere.

We paddle south around Hurtado Point, exit the populated area, and hug the cliffs along the coastline. The tide is just beginning to flood, and brilliant purple starfish cling to the rocks along the shore. The tidal surge is not yet significant, so our ride to Savary should be easy, particularly considering the light northwest winds. In fact, the marine forecast broadcasts an unusual report today for several of the local reporting stations – "sea calm." Marine reports of "sea rippled" are about as good as it gets, but "sea calm" is almost un-heard of.

After we reach the Iron Mine, it's time to start across to Savary. With July now ending, the flow of cruising boats to the north is still strong. But in a few weeks, the overall flow of cruisers will be to the south. Kayaks are considered speed bumps by these cruisers (especially those damn Americans), so we take a brief break as we drift gently and prepare for the push to Savary Island.

We depart the Iron Mine under full power, pushing across the open water, paddling strong. We point the nose of the kayak directly at Mace Point and thrust our paddles into the water with maximum effort. About a third of the way across, I yell forward to Margy that we should take a break. We float in nearly calm conditions and widely-spaced swells that provide a sea kayak with no difficulties. But a large cruiser is passing between the island and us, and his big wake is headed our way.

The wake is not enough to challenge us, but one wave swipes Margy's cockpit at an unusual angle and drenches her thighs.

"Damn Americans!" I yell as loud as I can muster. No one but Margy hears me, but it is worth the effort. It's probably a Canadian cruiser.

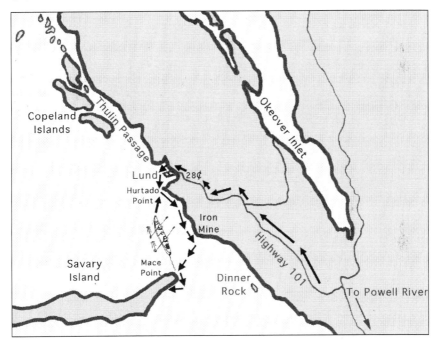

At Mace Point, we turn southbound and round the point to find a hoard of beach bums. The beach is strewn as far as we can see with umbrellas and people. Three children and their dad frolic near the point, reminding us that we are not far from civilization.

We beach the kayak in a sandy spot, clear of the large rocks. We don't have our swimsuits, but our nylon shorts allow us to wade waist-deep into the warm water. We'll dry off quickly in the sunny weather. It's a brief beach stop and a nice break. During our stay, the incoming tide is obvious. Judging by our kayak's nearly-floating position, the water is rising rapidly.

On the way back to Lund, we scoot nearly straight across to the harbor. Today, with little wind and minimal tidal effect, it's not necessary to go directly to shore at the Iron Mine. There are few kayak journeys that don't wear us out, but today's trip is an easy ride. And the nicely-fitting yellow life vest feels good.

Arriving back at Lund, we circumnavigate the harbor, finding some unique boats and a good view of Lund's new look. From here, the walkways looks peaceful, as tourists casually stroll along the shoreline. You can't see many of the parked cars.

We pass under the walkway from the water taxi office: scrape, crunch, scrape – oops, the flagpole on our stern catches the bridge. I turn just in time to see the flagpole whip back vertically – Sproing! Now we smoothly paddle around the fuel dock and back to the north launch ramp.

A 100-foot barge is angling toward the ramp, pushed by a small tugboat. We could probably beat him, but he is big, and we will need some time to pull our kayak from the water. So we paddle out of the way and watch him dock.

The tiny tug is chugging hard against the big barge, as the operator swings the wheel in full gyrations. Each turn of the wheel is perfectly timed to ease the barge into the ramp without any wasted motion. In comparison, Margy has been struggling for weeks with her new truck. Backing with our quad trailer in-tow is a difficult task, requiring repeated tries to get it right. But this guy never misses a beat pushing this giant barge into a spot tighter than typical for our trailer. With a full-tilt of the wheel to the right, and then a quick final swing to the left, the barge glides perfectly into place. You could almost drive the vehicles on without even lowering the loading ramps.

Now that the barge is safely docked, it is clear for us to bring our kayak ashore. It's an easy exit from here.

Of course, our yellow life vests make it more stylish. And a bit more expensive.

◊ ◊ ◊ ◊ ◊ ◊

# Chapter 18

# Clutch Kickin'

"Let's load the bikes today while I'm in town," I suggest. "It's really not a problem, even if the weather isn't good this weekend." I've reminded John that our 100cc motorcycles will be safe on my boat while parked at my cabin, and we'll be ready to go as soon as the weather breaks. Plus, I don't want to make a special trip to town just to load the bikes.

"Better wait," says John. "You never know what the weather is gonna do around here." This reminder is not the first. We have been doing battle over the subject for the past week. I want to load the bikes and be ready to travel to the Head as soon as the weather breaks. John has the same goal, but he doesn't give in regarding loading the bikes.

"Watch what happens when I call you on Friday, and we both have to drop everything to haul the bikes from the condo storage locker," I remind him of my weak argument. "And it will mean an extra trip to town for me."

"They could sit on the boat for weeks. This weather is totally unpredictable."

I'm insistent. So is John. One thing for sure: The bikes won't be loaded until John is ready. And he ain't ready yet.

We can only ride this route at the Head of Powell Lake on a weekend, when the logging shuts down. And the weather in the north is always worse than in the town, a product of mountain up-lift and the inland convection of the summer season. It's already the second week of June, and we've been waiting for the weather to cooperate for several weeks. It's just got to clear soon. Battling over the decision to load the boat keeps our dream alive. But John always wins such battles.

Yet this time I'm right. Of that I am sure. The Bayliner isn't going back to the chuck until we've completed this ride. I'm willing to wait weeks or even months. And if the weather breaks in the next few days, we'll wish we'd loaded the bikes.

The weather doesn't break. The bikes would have been a major nuisance aboard the boat for a full month, and John is right again.

* * * * *

There is one faint break in the weather, but it comes at the worst possible time. The weekend looks promising just as I get ready to leave for Los Angeles in late June. As I prepare to leave the cabin on Saturday, I have one last morning on the lake.

Early morning finds me fishing in First Narrows, right outside Hole in the Wall. It's not the fishing that has attracted me this morning. In fact, casting lures against the Narrow's cliff is merely a way to kill time while I await the boat from the south. John says it should pass here sometime after 8:30, and it's already 8:45. But the time schedule is not precise when you're hauling quads.

The Powell River ATV Club has chartered Bob's workboat to haul their quads to the Head this morning, and it should be quite a sight on the lake. Too bad we won't be with them.

Weekend morning traffic on the lake is typically minimal. I've sat at the Narrows for almost an hour now, and not a single boat has passed. But in the distance, a big boat is approaching, and it's moving faster than I expected. Usually, quads are barged to the Head, but today's boat is the largest workboat on the lake, an aluminum cargo ship with twin-diesels and a planing hull. I start the engine of my Campion to be sure I am in position for a good photo.

The workboat charges up the center of First Narrows at 25 knots. The wake from this fast, heavy vessel will be substantial against the cliff (and me), unless I run with the workboat, and that will allow me to get a better photo. Of course, taking a photo of a workboat in formation at close range while simultaneously trying to drive is asking a lot. But it's worth a try.

I am up on-plane quickly, and none too soon, for the quad hauler is blasting through the Narrows. Now I can see the details in the cargo bay. Seven quads are crowded into the aft area, two of them tilted up at a precarious angle, with their rear wheels protruding above the gunwales. One of the quads has a pole-mounted Canadian flag flying proudly in the 25-knot artificial wind.

I need full-throttle to keep up with the workboat, and boldly I edge closer. The workboat is a beautiful site, running on-plane only 50 feet from me. My head is poked out of the Campion's unzipped canvas hatch, my whole body leaning sideways for a photo, camera in one hand and the steering wheel in the other.

The lake is wonderfully smooth and cooperative, but an eye in the camera leaves no eye for any early morning logs that routinely populate this portion of the lake. Fortunately, it all comes off without a hitch, and I break off smoothly to the right, as the quad hauler blasts straight north. I reduce power to idle, watching the workboat dart away towards the Head. The wake hits and rolls me steeply from side to side, a reminder that I am left behind.

John is also left behind. Later that day we mutually admit that we hope the quad riders get a good ride, but deep inside there is the selfish hope that it rains like hell. We hate missing the opportunity.

It does rain like hell. The day in town is filled with scattered showers. At the head, the riders encounter pouring rain. That evening, it is too wet to set up their tents. Some of the riders crawl into the cabin of the boat, others into an abandoned trailer, in order to catch a few moments of fitful sleep. The next morning they ride in slightly improved weather with occasional showers, and they bring home lots of photos. Meanwhile, most of my photos of the quad hauling boat in-motion are nearly worthless blurs. It's one of those many cases of you-just-had-to-be-there.

A full month later, in late July, we are still waiting for our opportunity to ride our motorbikes at the Head. It's a good thing the motorcycles have not been sitting in my boat all this time. It would have been a frustratingly crowded six weeks, as John is quick to remind me.

But finally, we do load the bikes on the Bayliner on a Wednesday, and the weather looks promising for Saturday. On Friday, I am at my cabin with the bikes aboard, and ready to go except for one minor detail. My helmet and goggles are locked in my quad storage box at the airport. John has a key to every piece of Canadian equipment I own, except for the quad box, so I lament to him on the satellite phone that I'll have to ride without a helmet. It is a small motorcycle, not capable of much speed, but it distresses me to ride without a helmet. Safety is only part of the reason. Helmets provide a variety of comforting purposes, including bug protection and warding off errant branches that overhang the trails. Most quad riders wear helmets, and all motorcyclists wear them. Our small 100cc motorbikes could be considered the rare exception. But for me it will be very uncomfortable.

This is the first sign of a troublesome situation. The second sign occurs the moment John arrives at my cabin on Saturday morning, pulling into the rear dock in his Hourston and aptly kicking the ass of the boat around in his always-perfect parking maneuver. As he steps out of his boat, it starts to rain. It has been two full weeks of sunny skies, a rarity that has frustrated us. We need good weather to ride at the Head. We've been forced to squander endless sun for a series of complications in our personal schedules that have prevented us from hitting the Head while the weather is good. Now, at the very moment we are finally departing for our goal, the first drops of rain in weeks begin to fall. The brief shower ends quickly, but it is a strange sign that we note suspiciously, maybe even with a bit of apprehension.

The third sign is when I lose my hat overboard. We're struggling to get on-plane with the Bayliner's aft load of motorcycles, so I climb down from the command bridge and enter the cabin, crawling into the forward V-berth to shift my weight as far to the front as possible. I lay outstretched on the mattress, my head only inches from the bow. The water slaps hard on the hull below my head, the whack of 10-knot water on fiberglass. I hear the bow wave slowly moving aft, and now we are almost on-plane. John hits two quick toots of the horn, telling me we are on-speed.

Before leaving the V-berth, I unlatch the forward overhead hatch and open it against the resistance of the 20-knot cruise airflow. I poke my head up through the hatch and stare back at John on the command bridge. Good morning!

That's when my hat departs the scene. We quickly turn the boat and retrieve my beloved red Canada hat from the water, and we laugh about the seemingly mounting series of minor events. There's just something about this trip. A forgotten helmet, a few drops of rain, and a lost hat may not seem like much. But at the time, they strike me as warning signs, and the fact that I consider them as such is hard to digest. It is not my nature, nor is it John's, but we take the time to kiddingly discuss the events with a unique interest. Something somewhere seems to be speaking to us. We are listening, but we are not paying serious attention. Maybe warning signs are always like this.

\* \* \* \* \*

Our journey to the Head starts as a two-bike trip for John and me, but it has grown in the last few days into a group of riders, all intent on finding a rumored snow survey cabin near the Head. John has created a bit of hype about our riding plans, and others are now joining us.

As we pull into the logging dock at the Head, Bob's workboat is in the process of off-loading. It's a series of actions where everyone pitches in. This is the same boat I briefly rode formation with at First Narrows a month ago. This time the boat is carrying a lighter load – four large off-road motorcycles and a quad. The quad belongs to Bob, and the motorcyclists are friends of John. Mike and Luke join Doug and Mal (who are brothers), all highly experienced off-road motorcycle riders.

Bob is the only quad rider today, but it is not his original choice of transportation. In fact, today he wears a black jacket embroidered with "Motocross Champion, 2003," a remnant from his final year of Vancouver Island motorcycle racing competition. Today, he walks with a gimp as a result of his last motocross race. He was in first place on the next-to-last lap when he went airborne a little too high. He departed his 250cc Yamaha 30 feet above the ground, and came crashing down, wisely separated from his motorcycle. Both of his ankles fractured when he hit the ground. Thus, his forced transition to quads and a cane that accompanies him during hikes. He kids that he is a lot shorter these days.

I am nervous from the start. I haven't ridden my motorbike in a full year, and the controls are different from those on a quad. There's a clutch and kick-starter, and a series of gears that baffles me. It's up on the shift lever for second through fifth, and back down for first. Neutral fits somewhere in between, but finding neutral is something I've never mastered. I sit on the bike on the dock, thinking through the controls and switches, hoping I won't screw up severely in front of these expert riders. My small bike won't be able to keep up with theirs on the flat, nor can it climb as effectively. Add a few other items to the equation: my inexperience and lack of currency on bikes, John's adeptness on absolutely any piece of machinery (making a 100cc bike do 400cc work), and the fact that these riders want John to stay with them to tap his knowledge of these trails. Finally, add two other tidbits: multiple strange warning signs and no helmet.

My lack of a helmet is an immediate embarrassment. These strong riders all wear helmets and full protective body gear. Mal wears a chest contraption that reminds me of *Star Wars*. The lone American, on the other hand, challenges the Head without a helmet on his puny motorbike. He must think he is invincible, or maybe he is merely stupid.

I try to explain that this is the first time I have ever ridden without a helmet. It's a mistake, you see. Everyone nods, and I know they write me off as hopeless before the first engine is even started. There is an obvious weak link in today's ride, and we all clearly know who that is.

John comes over to see if all is okay. We're both struggling with our gear, since there is little room to carry anything on a bike. Our lunch and nearly everything else goes into our purposely-light backpacks. But John doesn't have a spot for his video camera. His bike carries our toolkit on the front, so he asks if I mind carrying his camera.

"Is it shock resistant?" I ask.

"Sure, and it's padded in this bag." The blue soft bag is a modified lunch case. We strap it onto the front of my bike with two bungee cords.

"Is it crash resistant?" I ask.

"Don't say that." It sounds like a warning. Bad luck or something. Maybe he is actually paying attention to the warning signs.

John goes back to his bike, and I prepare to get off to a good start. Go slow and sure. That's not the starter button (like on a quad) – it's the cut-off switch. The starter is a kick lever. I've made sure the bike is in neutral (always my most challenging task). I need to overcome compression of only 100cc's during the kick-start, as opposed to the kick needed for these high-compression bikes. It would be wonderful to demonstrate a start on first kick, so I make it a swift one.

But it's the shift lever.

These things happen. I hope no one notices.

I find the kick lever (on the other side) and give it a sharp push with my foot. The bike starts on first kick. I hope everyone notices.

As my bike warms up, I slide my backpack on. Doug comes over to see how I'm doing and immediately notices a problem.

"Hey, John, take a look at this!" He has to yell a bit, since John already has his earplugs in and is ready to kick-start his bike.

"It looks like the shift lever is bent," says Doug. He's one of those equipment nuts, like John, who would notice a crooked lever from fifty feet away. John kneels down beside my bike to inspect the shift lever.

"Man, I've never seen anything like that before," says John. "I wonder if it got smashed when we loaded it in the boat."

Now Mike is kneeling beside John, inspecting the damage. I didn't notice the bent lever when I kicked it by mistake, but there is no doubt what happened. I have a pretty strong foot.

I say nothing, but John uses a strong hand to strain against the lever and bend it back into position.

"That's a tough casting," says John. "Can't see how it could have bent like that." John is worried that the bent lever means the bike has been under structural stresses that may have damaged something else, so he carefully inspects the rest of the bike for damage. I decide not to tell him my foot has not modified the rest of the bike.

John looks up at me from his crouched position with a who-knows look on his face. I reply with my best who-knows return glance. Just one of those things.

It's another sign, and I know it.

\* \* \* \* \*

All four big motorcycles and the quad are well ahead of us immediately. The dust on the road behind them is an immediate problem. No helmet, no goggles, and the dust creeps under my sunglasses immediately. My eyes are watering, and I can feel tiny bits of grit in one of my eyes. Blinking only makes it worse, and keeping my eyes shut for more than a quick flick is not wise on a motorcycle. But John and I can ride side by side on the dirt road, minimizing the dust now that the other bikes are now far ahead.

After a few minutes, we find Mike stopped in the road, looking back over his shoulder at us. When we reach him, we stop, and he explains that four motorcycles and a quad can't stay close enough together to avoid self-imposed dust on this narrow road. So he has decided to drop back to ride with us. His big bike, however, makes me nervous in a three-abreast formation, so I slide back into the dust, and then even farther back to let the dust settle. It never really completely settles, but I'm sure I wouldn't even notice with helmet and goggles. After awhile, Mike takes pity on me (poor American) and lets me ride in front, while he trails behind a few feet.

We start up Falls Main, in search of the snow survey cabin. Bob and John have tried to find the cabin independently on previous rides, but an illusive shortcut to the cabin has not been found. There is a fairly obvious trail that neither of them have tried, primarily because it looks like a long hike. Surely there is a shortcut that is already marked with tape, if we can just find it.

We have traveled only two miles from the logging dock when we encounter our first real climb. The road is good, and I successfully downshift into first gear and make the hill with few problems. A short winding flat stretch and then another hill, only slightly larger than the first, follows this. I feel confident that all is well, although I fall considerably behind John and Mike on both hills. They take the climbs easily in second gear.

I enter the second hill with a good blast of speed on the flat in third gear, but now it's time to downshift. I kick down into second gear without a problem, and my bike slows gradually from there. Now it's time for first gear, so I kick down again. Suddenly I am in neutral. I can never find neutral when I need it.

I panic a bit, as my bike slows further on the moderate incline. I kick down hard to find first gear, and I find it, but my right hand twists the throttle too fast, and the bike's front wheel leaps upward a few inches off the ground. I know I must reduce the throttle, but I'm also sliding back in the seat and hanging onto the handlebars for dear life. My hand twists the throttle open even further and the front wheel comes high off the ground in a classic wheelie. John and Mike are already out of sight over the top of the hill as my motorcycle makes a perfect 180-degree pirouette, coming down solidly on the front wheel, with the bike facing straight downhill.

There is no hope, and I wisely (only because of natural instinct) leap off the bike to its left side, both hands still on the handlebars, guiding it as straight as possible downhill. I know I have to hit the cut-off button, and it is only a fraction of an inch from my right thumb, but I can't quite reach it. I stretch farther for the switch, but the bike is gaining momentum as gravity takes charge. I am running with the bike downhill. I must reach that button, and I'm almost to it. But time runs out.

I can't run any faster, and I can't reach the cut-off button. I let go of the bike and it careens off to the right side of the road, losing its balance without me to guide it. It smashes into the dirt. So do I.

Without the bike to hang onto, I am in free fall, full forward and face first. I try to hold my head up, and I think how wonderful it would be to have a helmet at this very moment. My face crunches into the dirt; I slide a few more feet, and come to a quick stop. I hear John running down the hill, yelling: "Hang on, Wayne! Hang on!"

This is very bad or really good. Nothing hurts. The bike engine quits by itself at the moment of impact. I lie prone on the ground, my face in the dirt.

Slowly, I raise my head and am pleased my neck moves. I open my eyes, and I can see, but I can feel the dirt on my face. I must have scraped it badly. It seems certain that blood is mixed with the dirt. I am fairly certain that part of my face is torn. But nothing hurts.

I instinctively glance sideways at the bike lying in the dirt. The blue bag with John's camera is still firmly attached. I'm elated.

John is hovering over me now, and I slide my backpack off and roll over on my back.

"Check your camera," I say. That's stupid, and we both know it. But I have to let John know that I've let him down, and I hope at least his camera came through this disaster unharmed. John protects every piece of equipment even remotely under his control as if it is his ordained duty. Right now, he doesn't care about the camera or even the bike. He's staring at my face.

"Your face is full of dirt. We need to wash it – carefully."

"I can do it myself. I've got some water. Does it look bad?"

"Well, I see some blood, mixed with a lot of dirt. How does it feel?" asks John.

"I think I'm okay. Take a look at your camera. And the bike."

"Check your knees first. They're always a problem when you fall like that." I'm convinced my knees are fine, and what are a few knee scrapes anyway? My face worries me.

"I'm okay, but I want to wash my face by myself." It's a stupid thing to say, but I have an overwhelming desire for privacy.

Mike is with me now too, and he notes that the bike has some battle damage but seems okay. John starts it after only a few kicks, and the frame isn't bent. In a few minutes, John and Mike retreat to the top of the hill. It may have been something I've said, but I think they instinctively know that I want some time to check out my face. I've got a clean pair of socks in my backpack to use as a rag and plenty of water.

I slowly and carefully wipe the dirt off my face and douse my cheeks and lips repeatedly with water. I can feel a few small cuts, hopefully no larger than they feel at first analysis. I have some anti-infection ointment in my backpack, and it feels cool on my wounds.

After a few minutes, John and Mike walk back down to me, and John says my face looks fine. He says there are only a few minor cuts, but I'm not sure I believe him. Only a little blood appears on my sock-rag. It could have been a whole lot worse.

"Have you checked your knees yet?" John asks.

"No, but they're okay." I'm standing now and looking down at my pants. Both knees of my pants are torn to shreds. I roll up my pant legs. John is right. My knees are a mess.

\* \* \* \* \*

We catch up with the rest of our group at a bridge on Falls Main. They have been waiting for us quite awhile, and I know they assume that the American is the source of the delay. They are right.

In our absence, they have scouted ahead for a shortcut to the snow survey cabin, but they have found nothing. There is an obvious trail adjacent to the bridge that leads upward towards where we think the cabin sits, but it isn't the short-cut. Everyone is ready to try it, but John wants to look at one more prospective spot first. It's a little farther up the road, where he saw trail marking tape in a swampy meadow on his previous trip up this road. John and I decide to check out this possible shorter route while the rest of the riders begin the hike from the bridge.

At the meadow, we find no trail marking tape. We walk a little ways into the clearing to see if we can find any semblance of a trail. The going is easy, except for the occasional swampy spot.

"Watch out here," says John as he steps about four inches into the mud as he tries to slide around a tree. I grab the trunk and try to step a little farther away from the muddy spot, but I misjudge. The mud comes up to my knee, and I feel water soak into my boot. It'll be a tough hike until that dries.

"What happened?" says John, when he sees my soaked pant leg.

"I missed," is my reply. "Another warning sign, maybe."

"Too late for that today," he replies. He's right.

We return to the road and ride back down to the bridge. The hiking trail upward is in excellent shape, probably more maintained by animal traffic than conscious human effort. There's lots of bear scat and several large bear paw prints.

We cross a well-maintained bridge, built particularly sturdy. Farther up the trail, a rope has been strategically anchored in the rocks to assist with the climb. The trail leads upward persistently, passing several waterfalls. Near one of these falls, we catch up with the trailing edge of the hiking group. Bob is bringing up the rear, hobbling admirably with his cane and two highly reworked ankles. He is struggling, but there is no doubt he will hike just as far as the rest of us today.

Well ahead of us, we hear a yell.

"That's Doug," says John. "He wouldn't yell like that unless he's found the cabin."

In another half-mile we are at the cabin, perfectly preserved since its original construction in 1938 as a snow survey cabin for the paper mill. The amount of snow pack is a critical factor in Powell

Lake's water level in the spring and the availability of waterpower at the dam and mill. The cabin still sports a sign proclaiming it is the property of Powell River Energy, but snow surveys these days are more efficiently accomplished by helicopter.

The cabin is constructed of huge yellow cedar logs, testament to the durability of this tough wood. Inside, the cabin is well organized and equipped to assist hikers who seek a fine shelter. As I sit on the outside deck, nursing my knees with ointment, Mike comes out with a shaving mirror he has found inside.

"Take a look," he says. "Your face is fine."

I am still concerned that my face is cut worse than the others say, and I'm pleased to see my tired image in the mirror. There are two obvious cuts, but nothing will need medical attention. It never ceases to amaze me how the mountain men of this region are so tough and independent, yet universally so caring. Even Americans receive their kindness of thought. But few of these tough guys would ever admit it.

* * * * *

After hiking back down from the cabin, we explore some of the side roads from Falls Main, viewing majestic waterfalls from protruding sheer cliffs, and we stop to play at a major granite rock washout. We push together on huge boulders, watching them crash downward along the steep granite face, sliding at first, and then picking up speed and crashing themselves into smithereens. We cheer as each boulder is overcome by the power of gravity and self-destructs. Mountain children at play in mindless games.

We transition back down Falls Main to Powell Lake, starting upward again on Powell Main. This road crosses the upper reaches of Powell River at several picturesque bridges and skirts the river at a variety of scenic spots. The beauty of the region is readily apparent here, and the granite cliffs and glaciers become even more plentiful as the road leads farther north.

A landslide crosses the road a few miles farther up the main. Alone and without a map, I would have guessed that the road simply ended at this rough spot of boulders and trees, but the reality is that gravity brought the surrounding terrain down in a thunderous wave of energy. To have seen or even heard this huge landslide would be a monumental memory.

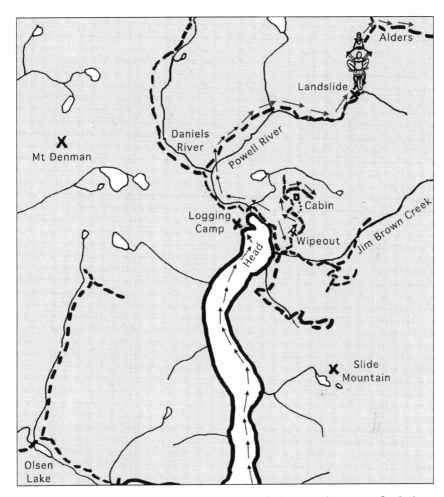

Looking more closely at the area of destruction, we find that others have already roughed out a route through the landslide. We improve on the entry point by adding some log ramps over the boulders, and then start through with our bikes. I make the mistake of slipping into the flow of bikes in the middle. I would have been better off last in line, since I stall my motorcycle several times at rough spots. This slows everyone behind me to a crawl, as they have to wait for me to move slowly through the makeshift trail. The American slows everyone down again.

The road returns to near-normal now, although it has received little activity from here northward in recent months due to the landslide. John says there are further landslides up ahead. I can hardly wait.

But we don't make it that far. In another few miles, the road is taken over by alders, pushing in from both sides. Other bikers have cut an occasional fallen log, allowing us to continue, but the thicket becomes a significant obstacle for all of us. The trail is still evident, but I can see only a few feet in front of me at most spots, leading to miscalculated routes and backtracking with more engine stalls.

As third in line, I push on, with John and Bob on the quad in front. Finally, they are ready to call it quits.

"Not worth beating ourselves to death any further," proclaims John. We wait a few minutes, but no other riders join us. They are probably smart enough to recognize this as an exercise in futility. Now we have to push back through the thicket, retracing the same tortuous route. At least some of the branches and bushes have been pushed aside by our trek in.

But it is still brutal. Another important reason to wear a helmet – branch protection. I'm used to ignoring small branches and bushes at the side of a trail on my quad. My helmet deflects these hanging obstacles with seldom a problem. Without a helmet, your head (and eyes) are exposed to everything. That includes bugs.

We rejoin the other riders at the first major bridge on the way back to the logging camp. It is sprinkling now, but the entire day of brooding skies has dropped almost no rain. Occasionally, showers have threatened, but never with an actual downpour. At one point, it felt like rain was beginning in earnest, but without my helmet I could tell that it was a dry rain – bugs rather than rain drops smacking at my face. Call it a bug shower.

At the bridge, we refill our water bottles from the crystal clear river. Bob offers to ride Luke's two-stroke Yamaha to evaluate the bike's mechanical condition, since Luke has been having problems today with fouled plugs, and Bob is obviously an expert regarding this model. He's probably also interested in seeing if he can still ride the same model of motorcycle that was the demise of his ankles. So they swap motorcycle for quad.

As we leave the bridge and start back down to the logging camp, I hear Bob behind me on the Yamaha. The two-stroke engine has a decidedly more intense winding RPM as it accelerates under Bob's experienced throttle hand. He's pushing the bike to its limits, but this is far from the intensity of motocross racing. By comparison, this is hardly a warm-up. All is under control.

Besides, Bob is smarter than me. He wears a helmet.

# Chapter 19

## Mylanta and Onions

The lake and the chuck are two of the primary focuses for Powell River. "Are you going up the lake?" is a question asked by locals as commonly as a city dweller might ask if you're going downtown. The lake is to the north of town. The chuck is to the south, extending farther to the southeast and northwest like a twisted letter-T.

One day at the grocery store, I grow tired of the question: "Do you have a card?" I'm not a member of the grocery store club, and it will be worth joining just to avoid the topic. As a bonus, I'll earn discount points as I shop and feel a bit more like a local. At checkout, I ask if I can have a card application, and the friendly female clerk offers to help me complete the required paperwork right on the spot. She insists in filling out the form for me, so I provide the pertinent data as she asks the questions.

"Phone number?" she asks.

"Well, I really don't have one."

"Not a problem," she replies. "Address?"

"Hole in the Wall on Powell Lake," I answer immediately. She hesitates a moment, and then starts writing.

"Okay, I don't think this information is important anyway. Here's your card," she says, peeling the gummed plastic card from the application. "They'll mail you the confirmation notice."

"Do you think my mailbox at Hole in the Wall will be filled with grocery ads?" I laugh.

"Probably not," she replies.

My address paints a clear picture for this grocery clerk, but I doubt the store's headquarters in Vancouver will waste their time trying to mail anything. A mailbox with an imaginary street address would be a cute touch in the Hole.

The distinct geographic indentation of the Hole in the Wall and its location near First Narrows invites the periodic annoying visitor, designated by Margy and me as the half-human breed called "Lookie-Loo." First Narrows is one-third of the way to the Head, with Second Narrows the two-thirds mark. Since few venture beyond Second Narrows, the Hole is considered the halfway point for many journeys. That makes it the ideal stopping point for a quick break (and a look). Turn into the hole, and motor back inside to see what's new and what's not.

Unfortunately, some boaters make this visit at full throttle. The narrow confines of the Hole then suffer boat wakes that are cussed by us: "Damn Lookie-Loo!" On summer weekends, the flow of traffic in and out of the Hole is both interesting and (at times) annoying. "Lookie-Loo!" is the constant cry from Margy or me.

One Saturday morning, a tin boat with two fishermen appears in the Hole. It cruises in slowly, the boat's occupants evaluating the bay carefully. I am eating lunch on the deck, and the boat seems to take forever to pass my cabin. My privacy is shattered. Then just as slowly, the boaters propel slowly out of the Hole, inspecting my float closely. I assume my floating garden is the object of their interest. The boat's driver looks like a gray-haired shriveled fisherman, and his only passenger is about sixteen years old. I envision them as grandpa and grandson on a fishing excursion.

Their boat finally disappears around the cliff, and then I hear the motor stop. A few minutes later, the two boaters reappear on the granite ledge, right below my favorite cliff observation site. I notice the stern of their boat protruding from the rocky curve in the shoreline, bobbing in a precarious mooring position against the cliff.

The young fellow wastes no time. He wears nothing but a pair of shorts, and he immediately dives off the cliff into the cool, deep water. He comes back to the surface yelling in excitement. The dive looks marginally safe from my perspective.

The older man, fully clothed in long pants and T-shirt, stares down at the water for at least five minutes, and then climbs down to a lower ledge. He focuses intently on the water below and then jumps cannon-ball style off the ledge. When the man surfaces, he too yells in excitement, even louder than the teenage boy.

I then realize why the boat entered and left at such a slow speed, inspecting my float. This pair probably comes here often when I am not home (no boat present), using my float, bridge, and rock wall stairs for access to the nearby cliffs. Today, they have to use a more ingenious approach to the cliffs for their diving adventure.

\* \* \* \* \*

It is Sunday afternoon when I call out to Margy: "Lookie-Loo! You gotta see this."

Maneuvering into the Hole from the main channel is the lake's largest houseboat, a rental craft that is often used by big groups. The houseboat is headed south toward the Shinglemill, home from a weekend's cruise on the lake, but now it is turning into the Hole. Even at full power this boat plows water at an exceedingly slow pace. It will take awhile for this vessel to get into the Hole. This is a grand tour for those aboard.

The houseboat passes abeam our cabin, with all hands on the top deck. I am hiding inside the cabin as they pass, peeking out through the kitchen window. There's something about shattered privacy on my float that bothers me. I prefer to remain hidden.

This group consists of Japanese tourists. I can hear them talking excitedly in their native tongue, their voices carrying clearly over the calm waters of the Hole, above the low rattle of the houseboat engine. Click, click, click go their camera shutters. Lookie-Loos extraordinaire.

* * * * *

I sit on the couch inside my cabin, a solo morning on the float. The sun has just topped Goat, and the quiet of the new day engulfs me. I savor my coffee and scan an astronomy observer's guide. The previous night raised some mysteries that are best solved in the daylight. Turning on lights during a nighttime observing session to read the fine print in a book can destroy an amateur astronomer's night vision, so many of the unknowns are tucked away for research the next day.

Now I am reading about M31 and M110 – the Andromeda galaxy and its companion. Both galaxies were visible last night in the same field of view at low magnification. And, yes, that was definitely M32, blazing like a fuzzy star, not far from M31. Three galaxies in a tiny chunk of sky, all gravitationally bound together.

Suddenly, a vicious cat fight erupts on the rear deck! I know cats, and it sounds like a nasty fight. But there are no cats here. The brutal screams continue – shrieks and squeals, interspersed with brief periods of silence. My heart races. What animals are here? Should I close the glass patio door? The screen door is all that separates me from this ferocious altercation.

A combination of curiosity and hope draws me toward the door. Maybe I can stop these critters from destroying each other. My laceless shoes slip on quickly as I exit to the deck. A kayak paddle from the den serves as my defensive weapon.

As I round the corner of the cabin, two otters the size of large dogs are paddling swiftly away. Their matted brown coats shine in the low sunlight. Both look over their shoulders at me. The lovers' spat is over.

The previous week on the deck of John's Number 2, I watched Bro play the part of a madman as he went into a sudden barking fit, accompanied by pacing back and forth. He broke into a run on the short float deck, skidding to a halt only to resume his acceleration in the opposite direction. Bro paused and frantically sniffed between the cracks in the decking, and resumed his barking.

"Otters," said John. "They live under the float, and Bro smells them."

I hadn't considered the possibility that otters might inhabit my own under-float foundation. I had never sighted an otter in the lake's waters.

Maybe this fighting pair lives under my float. Could these otters be the source of critter noises that shake my confidence during nighttime telescope sessions? And what about Margy's USO incident? Would an otter grab the foot of a human swimming near its territorial side of the float? The south end is usually free of swimming activity. Maybe one of these otters saw Margy's foot dangling below our deck at this end of the float and chose to go after it. Not a pleasant thought.

I consider this for a few minutes and make a quick decision. Margy's USO incident is less scary when remembered as a confrontation with an ancient friendly sea creature than a modern otter with an ugly disposition. I decide not to tell her about today's lovers' quarrel. Little white lies have their place.

Local remedies are normally the best, and there are plenty of local prescriptions on Powell Lake.

On a sunny summer day at John's Number 1, major beach maintenance is in progress. When I arrive, John's brother, Dave, and his wife, Jayne, are assisting John in the movement of giant boulders and logs in a beach improvement project. For nearly an hour, I help them move the large obstacles to more picturesque locations. The boulders can be moved quite easily once they are in the water, their buoyancy making our small bodies simulate Tarzan.

The logs are a bigger problem, since they are jammed onto the beach, their dry weight beyond the power of any one person. Working together, we make a little progress. Jayne, the daughter of a logger, can push a mean log. She also seems to have a local remedy for any physical ailment.

When I was previously bothered by a rash of mosquito bites from reading in bed near a screenless window (and an overhead light for added mosquito attraction), Jayne recommended Mylanta as a cure for the itchy bites. Dab a drop of the liquid antacid on the bite, and it provides instant relief from the itching. Your body looks like a disaster zone with patches of powdery dry Mylanta, but it sure takes care of those bites.

Today, Jayne is lifting logs on par with the rest of us, helping heft the timber over rock obstacles and into the water. From the water, we can maneuver the logs into their new beachfront decorative locations.

As we try to lift a particularly large log, Dave yells "Hornets!" but remains firmly standing at the site of the aerial attack. In fact, he holds onto the log, although wasps are exiting a nest within the wood in large numbers. I see the swarming hoard and turn to run. Before I move more than a few feet, a wasp immediately stings me – right in my chest. In fact, the sting is strategically located only a fraction of an inch from my nipple, and it hurts intensely. I actually think I might pass out from the pain, but I sit down on the beach (a long ways from the wasp nest) and try to regroup my energy.

As I attempt to gather my strength, I watch Dave continue to work near the log, wasps swirling around him, while the rest of us retreat farther down the beach. Dave is totally unafraid of the wasps, and they apparently know and respect him for it. As he continues to move the log (single-handed movement is slow), he provides an ongoing commentary to us regarding wasps. Neither bees nor wasps have ever stung him, since he always takes the tact of consciously relaxing around them.

Wasps know when someone is afraid, he says, by the person's rapid movements, and that's when they sting. As he talks about his immunity to such bites, the wasps swarm around Dave's head and chest as he continues to tug on the log.

Meanwhile, Jayne informs me that I don't look so good (no surprise to me), and suggests that I go back to my cabin, lie down, and try to relax. A wasp bite can be treated with a raw onion, of course. Doesn't everyone know that?

When I arrive at my cabin, I am exhausted. I feel at least as pale as I probably look. The wasp sting is throbbing worse than ever, and my upper chest is now considerably swollen. What a place for an insect bite.

I cut a large onion and place its flat face on my chest. There is instant relief. The onion feels cold against my skin, and the pain is being pulled from my chest. I sigh in relief. When I remove the onion, the pain of the sting returns. But placing the onion against my chest once again provides a wonderful coolness, and I can feel the pain pouring from my flesh.

It is only a temporary remedy, since the pain returns each time I remove the onion. But that is of no concern. I sleep with the onion taped to my chest, having pleasant dreams, and awakening to a day with no further discomfort. Local remedies, undocumented on bottles of Mylanta and the skin of onions, are always the best.

◊ ◊ ◊ ◊ ◊ ◊ ◊

# Chapter 20

# Sneakin' Up on Bears

As I step onto the deck to evaluate the middle-of-night weather, First Narrows echoes the effects of the wind to the south. The North Sea must be churning to a frenzy, based on the river-like sound of the Narrows. It is 1 AM, and the darkness provides rushing sounds, like water tumbling over a giant waterfall, but it is only the wind waves to the south reflected through the Narrows. The Hole is nearly calm, but the marine report indicates strong southeasterlies, forecasted to shift to the southwest during the night, with clearing skies to follow.

I walk onto the dock extension where the Bayliner is tied. The boat is bobbing a bit, and one of the aft fenders repetitiously crunches against the dock. Two 100cc motorcycles are secure in the rear of the boat, and all is ready to go for the planned trip. John and I have plans to ride on logging roads that connect to Powell Lake. It's BC Day, so these roads will be wide open for us to ride.

Our options are limited, since most of the roads we can access from the lake are short, and each entails a lot of work offloading and onloading our bikes for a brief ride. Goat Island itself is a big ride, but we explored those roads the previous summer, so that isn't on today's riding list. John is reluctant to try the shorter rides, since he is in his too-much-work mode, but I convince him to set Monday aside for two brief trips, one up Beartooth Main and the other ride on the far east end of Powell Lake.

After listening to the wind and waves and watching the fast moving clouds overhead, I manage to get a few more hours of sleep. But I instinctively awaken at 4 AM to check the weather again. Now the winds are moderate in the Hole, but that's a good thing. Just as forecasted, the wind is gusty from the southwest and the sky is rapidly clearing. The cold front has passed

After another short nap, the gentle rocking of waves awakens me at 6 AM. That's the normal hour for crummy boats to pass northbound through the Narrows, taking loggers to their morning work sites. But it's a holiday. Several more workboats follow a few minutes later. It looks like it is not only a workday – it's a major logging day on the lake.

Now wondering if we are going riding today, I decide that another nap is futile. So I begin to fix my sandwich and snacks in the summer morning twilight for a day of riding, optimistically hoping I get to eat lunch on the trail.

* * * * *

John pulls into the Hole at about 9 AM, swings around the breakwater, and heads for his preferred parking spot behind my cabin. I'm there to grab his lines as he adeptly turns his boat into the parking spot on the kayak dock behind the firewood float. It's a tight squeeze, but John expertly kicks the ass around, and the boat stops perfectly parallel to the dock and about a foot away. He never ceases to amaze me.

"Lot's of workboats this morning," I state, expecting to surprise John. The boats were at their destinations long before John got out of bed.

"Not a problem," says John, not flinching a bit.

"But there were a ton of them headed north," I clarify. "Maybe it's not a holiday for logging."

"That's the mechanics. They work on holidays, since it's a good time to get caught up on maintenance."

How does he know this stuff? But I'm not surprised.

"Was it rough in the North Sea?" I ask.

"Not really. The lake is in pretty good shape. And it looks like a good day for riding."

The wind has now shifted to the northwest, the cold front well past and rushing inland. A few puffy cumulus clouds dot the horizon, with otherwise clear skies and perfect weather for riding.

* * * * *

John spots the boats at the Beartooth dock long before I do. When I am finally able to see a single dot at the dock, he counts two boats and identifies them as workboats. It's a small logging dock, so John is concerned with parking space.

As we pull into the boomed area, it is apparent that the only remaining spot is tightly nestled near shore. John drops me off at the end of the dock, and I prepare to receive the Bayliner at the tight near-shore spot. He angles in perfectly, and the boat drifts precisely into the spot. It's like parallel parking a locomotive, but John does it on the first try.

The ramp to shore drifts in the water near the lake's edge, making us wonder where the workers from the boats have gone.

"They probably aren't here," says John. "Beartooth hasn't been logged in months. I bet another boat picked them up."

After retrieving the ramp from the water, we are able to push our motorbikes to shore and get ready to ride. It's already so warm that I strip to my T-shirt. It's not the best way to ride, since long sleeves better protect your body from scrapes, but it's too nice today not to be tempted. But I stay in long pants and wear my helmet – I've learned those essentials the hard way.

As soon as we clear the lakeside turnout, it is obvious that we are the only humans to climb this road recently. In only a few months, the main has been overtaken in spots by alders. The road is still easy to ride on our bikes, but it won't remain so for long. Nature has begun her quick reclamation of the wilderness.

I begin to visualize where we are going today. Beartooth is one of the landmark mountains of the region. Its name is appropriate, as the sharp granite peak rises precipitously from the lake. Beartooth Main is a steep climb, but it is limited to the tamer side of the mountain. About halfway up the main, a 2-mile hiking trail to the top begins. It's a steep trail that even John has not climbed. I've talked to people who have climbed Beartooth, and they universally consider it the most challenging climb of their life. We'll only be riding today, but it will be on a road that no one has probably touched for months. I feel like a frontier explorer, and there is a sense of special secrets in the air.

We climb in a series of switchbacks, exploring some of the dead-end roads that lead into the slashes. It is not an easy climb, with branches and rocks strewn everywhere. At one spot, a huge stump has fallen into the middle of the road, like a tree with a road built around it. We navigate around the stump, and John stops at a spot where a dozen small boulders have accumulated in the road. He clears one that is particularly in our way, and I stop behind him to wave in thanks over the noise of my engine.

To the sides of the road, water tumbles over granite cliffs. Glacier fields speckled with ice mingle with forested slopes. Majestic views cap a glorious day, with no visible sign of humanity to spoil the essence of isolation.

\* \* \* \* \*

**W**e are onloaded and motoring away from the Beartooth dock by early afternoon. Our destination is Narrows Main at the east end of the lake. We often ride near the narrowing neck of Powell Lake on the south side where Rainbow Main joins Goat Main, but the north side of the lake is unreachable on our quads.

The dock is empty and so is the road from the lake. Like Beartooth, Narrows Main is encroached by bushes, with alders quickly reclaiming portions of the road. There is no danger of logging trucks or any other vehicle here, so we ride side-by-side.

"Feels like Chippewa," I yell to John over our engines.

"It does!" He smiles back at me in respect for my accurate observation. Like the road along Chippewa Bay, this road possesses the same dry nearly-flat landscape. But soon we are climbing into more interesting terrain. The road climbs through older trees and a rapidly thickening forest.

I ask John to stop at a spot where we can hike off the road into the forest. Since most of the roadside trees are in rugged ground, he picks a spot near a creek for us to venture into the forest.

As we climb upstream along the creek, we encounter a fallen old-growth tree and climb on top of it. The tree's trunk is all that remains of this giant, but it is solid and straight as we walk on it for nearly a hundred feet. It is covered with thick moss, and underneath the moss is a 2-inch layer of black soil that has been created from the decaying wood. It is a memorable walk on top of an old giant.

Back on Narrows Main, we climb high into a slash that looks out onto Powell Lake. We stop for another lunch (our second today) in a huge slash that has left old-growth stumps protruding prominently along the side of the road. The sun beams brilliantly down on us, and the temperature hovers near uncomfortable warmth. The day is magnificent and has treated us well.

As we descend down the main, John leads me on a spur that turns eastward towards Goat Lake. We travel along Goat River on the side I have never seen before and gaze across to Rainbow Main. Further east, we look down on Goat Lake and Goat Main on the other side.

"There's a quad," says John. He's not talking about hearing a quad. He sees one on Goat Main. I search for the bike but can't see it.

"Check up there," says John, pointing to a clearing where the main climbs towards Windsor Lake. "He'll be in that area soon, so you should be able to see him. Look for the dust."

Sure enough, a few seconds later, I see a small cloud of dust in the clearing. Looking closer, I can identify it as a quad weaving along Goat Main.

"He's just bustin' along, enjoying it," says John. "Might be Jack."

"Why do you think it's Jack?" I ask.

"Well, I don't know for sure, but it looks like him, and I think he's driving Goat Main today."

Now how does he know this? Quads all look alike from such a distance. I bet he's right though.

We leave our observation spot and find a new location where we can see up Goat Lake nearly to the end. The view is impressive – walls of granite that drop steeply to the lake. I try to capture it in my camera. It's the kind of view that cannot be properly seized in a shutter.

On our way back to the boat, John cuts his engine at the top of a hill and begins to coast down the grade. Riding beside him, I follow his lead and hit the "kill" switch on my motorcycle, coasting with the clutch engaged. I assume we are just saving fuel and enjoying the quiet.

"We'll sneak up on the bears," says John. It might work.

We continue to coast for about a half-mile and then pop the clutch to restart our bikes. I stall my engine, of course, but I catch up with John farther down the nearly level road. Suddenly, John guns his engine beside me and takes off like a rocket.

"Bear!" yells John.

I see the huge bear just as John yells, and now I am accelerating behind him down the nearly-straight road. The bear is winning the race, although John is up to speed now, and the bear isn't leaving the road. I am amazed at how fast this huge animal can run.

My mind is engaged at high speed now, and I wonder if chasing a bear is a wise idea. The answer is too obvious to acknowledge.

John is in front of me, and in front of John is the bear. It is a futile chase. The road ends in about a half-mile at a slash, and I watch the bear bound up a rocky, steep slope. He is gone in a flash, just as we come to a screeching halt.

The bear easily wins the race. I figure that is fortunate for all three of us.

# Epilogue

## On the Phone

I have been sitting in the waiting area at the California Department of Motor Vehicles for a almost a half-hour, and the scrolling-text sign tells me those without appointments will have to wait even longer ("Non-Appointments, Pomona, wait time 57 minutes"). I guess I should be thankful. Another sign says: "No credit cards accepted." But they take checks – go figure. Since I seldom carry checks, it's fortunate I have cash today.

My stay in California has exceeded two weeks, and I am completely wound up by now. But there is hope. If I can get the VORs in my Piper Arrow fixed this week, I'll be airborne to Canada in a few days.

It's not that I hate California. Los Angeles is a wonderful place, with the late summer weather leading to endless sun and moderate temperatures. There is good absolutely everywhere. But, still, this isn't British Columbia.

My appointment number is F032, and an automated voice calls new numbers every few seconds. Mine isn't one of them.

The sign on the wall is a classic: "Please do not place children on the counters." This place is full of children running wild. Maybe they'd settle down if they sat on the counters.

\* \* \* \* \*

As soon as I return home with my renewed driver's license, I call John. It is the middle of the day, and I am surprised and thankful to find him home.

He has received the photos I mailed to him last week, and he particularly likes the one of us loading our motorcycles onto the Bayliner and the picture of Jack on his quad in the Eldred River, well above his hubcabs in water.

John also likes the photo of himself that he asked me to take – inside a huge drainage pipe under Narrows Main. John likes photos that show scale. I remind him of the unique shot he took of Eldon at the head of Jervis Inlet in front of an old-growth tree. John and Eldon boated there and road motorcycles as far as the rugged terrain would allow them to go (not very far). In the photo, Eldon's hands are fully outstretched; yet, the tree trunk's diameter outreaches his arm-spread by nearly double. There is talk about building a road from Powell River to Squamish along this route – yeah, right.

John installed a barrel under the corner of my firewood float this week. The float was riding low in the water after my last load of firewood. At present, the corner is again above the waterline, but now the float needs a barrel on the other side. It's a never-ending balancing act.

The rotten boards on my transition float and stairway to the outhouse have been replaced with new cedar planks. I had placed a call-in order for the project, providing the exact dimensions of the bad boards. John appreciates exactness. It was a bit like ordering a pizza to-go.

John didn't go riding last week, and he's grumpy about it. But he couldn't pass up an offer from Rick to help build new stairs from Number 2 to the quad parking area above his cabin. The old access to this area was via a granite and wooden vertical ladder that was meant for occasional climbing only. Now Bro won't need a severe ass-push to get him up to the parking area. With the Last Chance Trail through the Bunsters now open for business, the "business" will include John's brothers and friends, en route to Number 2. John's generosity to others never ends, but I predict he will regret opening the land route to Hole in the Wall. Pretty soon, we'll be fighting off the ATV tourists. In reality, I know it will work out fine, but the encroachment of humanity into my paradise is always a fear. Who says it's my paradise?

The fanbelt replacement project on the Bayliner has been de-layed, since the new belt was the wrong size. It will require another trip to Number 3 later this week, and then the boat will go back into the chuck under's John's supervision. The Bayliner will await me in Westview Marina next week, ready to head north towards Bute Inlet. I've never been on the chuck during September and October, so this is an adventure that catches my mental focus. In fact, as soon as John mentions "Bute," I'm ready to ignore the Arrow's VOR problems and launch for Canada. I visualize the stream of American boats headed south (home) as the summer ends, and me headed north. It paints a nice picture.

After twenty minutes on the phone, I feel that the transition has already begun. I can feel myself winding down, and I'm not even home yet. But soon...

◊ ◊ ◊ ◊ ◊ ◊ ◊

# About the Author

On the Trail in Theodosia Valley

Wayne Lutz previously was Chairman of the Department of Aeronautics at Mount San Antonio College in California, leading the school's Flying Team to championships seven times as Top Community College Flying Team in the United States. He also served as a California Air National Guard C-130 aircraft maintenance officer.

The author is a flight instructor with 7000 hours of flight experience. In the past two decades, he has spent summers in Canada, exploring remote regions with his Piper Arrow and camping next to his airplane. In 2000, he discovered Powell River, British Columbia.

The author resides in a floating cabin on Canada's Powell Lake and in a city-folk condo near Los Angeles. His writing genres include regional Canadian publications and science fiction. His next book, *Up the Strait*, is scheduled for publication in June 2006.

# *www.PowellRiverBooks.com*

# Powell River Books Ltd.
# Powell River BC

Cabin Number 3, Hole in the Wall
Powell Lake, **British Columbia**

*Up the Main* is the 2nd is a series of volumes
focusing on the unique geography and
people of coastal British Columbia

**Books & Photo CDs**

Order at: *www.PowellRiverBooks.com*

## Up the Lake

## Up the Main

## Up the Strait

### Reader's can email the author:
wlutz@mtsac.edu

ISBN 141207218-2

9 781412 072182